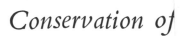

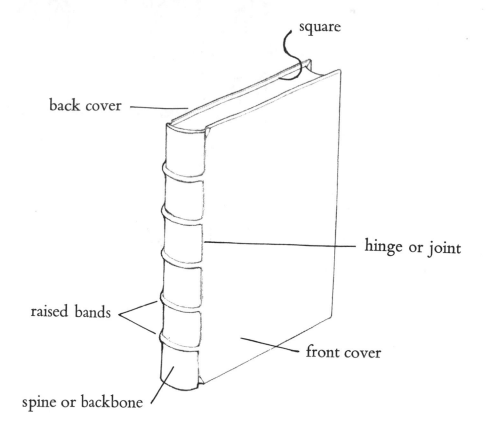

square

back cover

hinge or joint

raised bands

front cover

spine or backbone

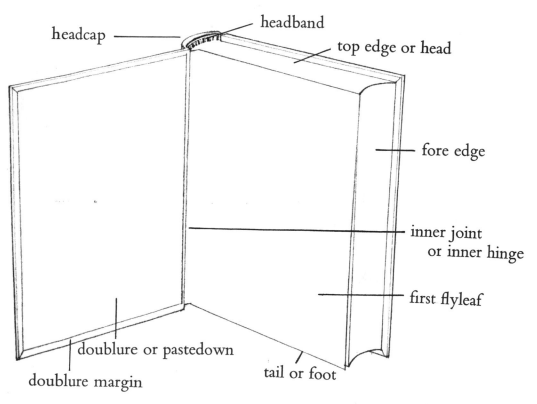

headcap

headband

top edge or head

fore edge

inner joint
or inner hinge

first flyleaf

doublure or pastedown

doublure margin

tail or foot

Parts of a hand-bound book

PAMPHLET 1 OF A SERIES

Cleaning and Preserving Bindings and Related Materials

Second Edition, Revised

By Carolyn Horton

Illustrated by Aldren A. Watson

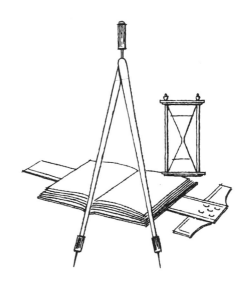

Library Technology Program
American Library Association
Chicago

Second Printing 1973

Horton, Carolyn.
    Cleaning and preserving bindings and related materials.
Illustrated by Aldren A. Watson. 2d ed., rev. Chicago,
Library Technology Program, American Library Associa-
tion ₍1969₎

    xx, 87 p. illus. 28 cm. (LTP publication, no. 16. Conserva-
tion of library materials, pamphlet 1)

    Bibliography: p. 73–81.

    1. Books—Conservation and restoration. ɪ. Title. (Series:
American Library Association. Library Technology Program. LTP
publications, no. 16. Series: Conservation of library materials,
pamphlet 1)

Z701.H79 1969   025.7   76–95200
SBN 8389–3008–5   MARC

Library of Congress   70 ₍3₎

Standard Book Number 8389-3008-5 (1969)

Library of Congress Catalog Card Number: 76-95200

Copyright 1967, 1969 by American Library Association

Printed in the United States of America

Contents

Illustrations

Foreword

Librarians generally are not well informed about the preservation and repair of library materials. Formal professional training in binding and restoration is not given in this country, and even informal instruction is available only in large metropolitan centers. Publications on the subject do not provide the detailed and authoritative information necessary for unskilled people to perform conservation activities. As a consequence, preservation and restoration work in libraries is usually done by people with insufficient training and skill in conservation techniques.

From its very early days, the Library Technology Program has been interested in a project that would result in a manual on the conservation of library materials. In the fall of 1965, the Council on Library Resources, Incorporated, made a grant to finance the planning phase of a project which it is hoped will produce a series of pamphlets on the preservation and restoration of library materials. The proposed series will cover the care and repair of ordinary books and pamphlets, the preservation and restoration of rare books, and the conservation of all other types of materials collected by libraries and individuals.

Because the primary purpose of the project is to provide a manual that will be useful to people unskilled in the practice of conservation, all sections devoted to techniques will be given detailed treatment. Each pamphlet will be illustrated to clarify points in the text. Bibliographies will be included. Laboratory evaluations of conservation techniques and materials that are carried out in conjunction with the preparation of certain sections will be reported.

In October, 1965, the Advisory Committee for this project held its first meeting and drafted an outline for the proposed manual. The committee also considered a number of specialists who might be commissioned to write on various subjects. It was decided that the first publication should be used as a pattern for subsequent topics.

In December, 1965, Mrs. Carolyn Horton of New York, a hand bookbinder and an expert in the field of conservation of library collections, agreed to write the first publication. Aldren A. Watson, who has a keen interest in hand bookbinding, was commissioned to prepare illustrations for the pamphlet, and Greer Allen, director of the Printing Department, The University of Chicago, agreed to design and supervise its production.

During 1966, as part of the preparation of Mrs. Horton's essay, seventeen products used to clean and restore bookbindings were tested by Walter C. McCrone Associates, Chicago, with respect to their safety for use on book materials. The procedures used in these tests and the principal conclusions drawn from them are summarized on pages 62–64.

Mrs. Horton's pamphlet was originally published in September, 1967, as LTP Publication No. 12. It has proved to be one of the Library Technology Program's most popular publications, and it soon became evident that a new printing would have to be made. For this second edition, the author has made a number of changes in the text, expanded and updated the bibliography, added a work flow diagram, and made certain necessary changes in the list of supplies and equipment. In addition, slight modifications have been made in some of the illustrations, and an index has been added.

We feel that the author has, over a period of many years of experience, developed highly efficient methods and procedures for the refurbishing of book collections—including the marking of disintegrating books for attention, the attachment of loose materials, the cleaning of books, and the application of leather preservatives—and has described these methods and procedures here with admirable clarity and precision. She has also included a very useful appraisal of leather preservatives and other materials used in conservation. It is hoped that this new edition will prove even more useful to librarians, conservators, and private collectors throughout the world.

HAROLD W. TRIBOLET
Chairman, Advisory Committee
Conservation of Library Materials

Editorial Preface

Every library—large, small, public, private, academic, or special— should have a well-defined program for conserving the materials which it houses. The cost of such a program can be a sizable part of the library budget, but a program is essential if libraries are to accomplish their ultimate goal, that is, bringing library materials to library users.

Libraries acquire and preserve printed materials—books, pamphlets, broadsides, maps, etc.—to meet a potential informational or recreational need. It is the responsibility of the librarian, or book owner, to maintain these materials in such physical condition that they will be available for immediate use. Whenever materials can no longer be safely used because their general physical condition has deteriorated to a point where restoration or replacement is necessary, the librarian, or book owner, has an obligation to make the material serviceable as quickly as possible.

An effective conservation program is not a simple matter. It is one thing to agree to the general principle that library materials require treatment when they are in such physical condition that they cannot be used satisfactorily by readers. It is quite another to decide what kind of treatment is best for a specific item in order to preserve it in usable form. For example, books show evidence of wear and tear most frequently at the head and foot of the backstrip, at the hinges, and at the four outer corners. When such damage is observed, one's first reaction is to replace the badly worn headcap, to repair the split outer hinge, or to recover those corners where the fabric has worn through to the boards. And yet it is quite conceivable, and even probable, that many books evidencing such wear and tear are still quite serviceable. If they are used seldom or not at all, they can be left on the shelves as they are for months, years, or even decades, without sustaining further serious damage.

On the other hand, books may show little or no sign of physical wear and appear to be in excellent condition when, in fact, they will begin to fall apart as soon as readers start to use them. In such cases, the books were probably printed on inferior paper and bound with poor-quality materials whose chemical deterioration has been very rapid. Such books, if at all valuable, require immediate treatment to prevent further deterioration.

While these two unusual cases illustrate the difficulties encountered in deciding whether a particular library item needs restoration, generally the question of "what" to conserve is not so difficult to answer. Certain guidelines can be set down for the selection of library materials that require some degree of conservation ranging from simple furbishing and minor repairs through major repairs, binding, rebinding, restoring, and extra-fine binding. There are, in fact, three broad criteria for selecting materials for conservation work. These criteria have to do with the importance, or significance, of the item to the library and the library patron. They are (1) Use: How much use and/or abuse is the material likely to sustain? (2) Replaceability: How easily and economically can the material be replaced? and (3) Value: How rare, special, or valuable is an item?

In every library there are some books that are heavily used, others that are less frequently but regularly used, and many that are seldom, if ever, taken from the shelves. For example, in public libraries, heavily used materials include reference books, such as dictionaries, encyclopedias, almanacs, the various annual compilations, textbooks assigned as required reading, and current fiction and non-fiction, especially those titles on best-seller lists. Such materials must be stoutly bound in order to withstand heavy use and abuse. In this instance a durable binding is essential.

At the opposite extreme, there are, particularly in research libraries, large quantities of materials that are used infrequently but that must be preserved so that they can circulate when needed. For such items, a chemically stable binding which will permit long-term storage on the shelves is far more important than a strong one.

Between these two extremes of use, there are, especially in college, university, and research libraries, vast amounts of materials that have been used steadily over a long period and that are likely to continue to be used five, ten, and even a hundred years from now. While they do not sustain heavy use and abuse in a short time, they do become worn and damaged and eventually require replacement or restoration.

From the foregoing, it should be evident that the person responsible for preservation, who is sometimes called a conservator, must have some idea as to how heavily or lightly the materials are used in order to make an informed decision as to whether it is necessary to repair, restore, or replace such materials.

Not only must the librarian, or book owner, decide how much an item is used, or is likely to be used, he must also consider how difficult and costly it would be to replace it. If replacement is easier and more economical than conservation, then replacement would usually be advisable. For example, some book titles are available in print over a very long period of time; the cost of new copies of these titles is low when compared with the cost of repairing and rebinding a badly worn copy already in the library. A case in point is a popular Charles Dickens novel which is likely to be in print in an inexpensive edition.

Another type of material that may be easily and economically replaced is that which is available in microform reproductions. Micro-transparencies, microfiches, and micro-opaques have proved to be excellent media for the storing of many kinds of useful—but infrequently used—library materials. By these means, the librarian can have on hand valuable source material for those users who need it and at the same time be freed of the necessity and responsibility for maintaining large quantities of such materials in their original form.

However, when useful materials are so difficult or expensive to acquire that replacement is impractical, then the librarian, or book owner, must preserve as best he can those items that are already in the library collection. This situation is becoming more and more common because of the growing demand—and consequent rising costs resulting from diminishing supply—for scarce and out-of-print items. In spite of the difficulties, however, a librarian, or book owner, can arrive at a reasonable decision regarding replacement.

Finally, in selecting books for repair and preservation, a judgment often must be made regarding the value of material in the collection. A large, well-established research collection may include many materials that fall into the category of items that are of considerable value—possibly priceless or irreplaceable. Some items will be deemed worthy of their special status because of their uniqueness; others will be treasured because they have aesthetic value; still others will be preserved for sentimental reasons. Examples of such items are first editions, the rare artifact (a jewel-encrusted, fourteenth-century bound volume), autographed copies, association copies (for example, an item given by the author to a library's principal benefactor), or the first book bought for a library. Whatever the reason for assigning an unusual value to an item in the library, this value is nonetheless real and must be reckoned with. It is on the basis of such value that some library materials will be selected for special care and protection.

Once the decision has been made as to what to conserve, on the basis of usage, replaceability, value, or a combination of these factors, it is then necessary to decide what sort of conservation treatment each item should receive—how extensive and expensive the repair and restoration of the material should be.

In this connection, handling restoration problems would be relatively simple if books were uniform as far as materials used in their manufacture were concerned. However, such uniformity is not a reality in the world of books. While bookmaking is basically the same from volume to volume, each book which must be repaired is a problem by itself. It may be old or new; it may be unbound, bound, or rebound; if bound, it may be bound with paper, or paper-covered boards, or cloth-covered boards, or leather, or a combination of any of these. The paper on which the book is printed may be poor, average, or good.

In any case, the problems to be faced in restoring individual books manufactured or produced under varying circumstances with a variety of materials in different ways require special solutions in most instances.

With each book with which the conservator works, the special restoration problems that have to be solved also will depend upon other factors besides the methods and materials used in its making. For example, when an incunabulum in a deteriorating, inappropriate, mid-nineteenth-century binding by an anonymous binder is in need of a new binding, it is usually considered more sensible to construct a new binding in fifteenth-century style rather than to repair or reproduce the present binding. Certainly the conservation of such an item must be planned on the basis of doing the job well enough and beautifully enough to last centuries—not simply years or decades.

In the conservation of rare books, the craftsmanship of the book-binder and the quality of his materials are of the first importance. The goal is to restore the material to a condition equivalent to, or better than, its original state. But even in those instances where the book does not require such special conservation treatment, the conservator will still have to determine what sort of treatment books and other materials selected for conservation will receive, and he will finally have to base this decision on the value of the item as well as on the manner of its use.

In summary, a librarian, or book owner, selecting library materials for conservation must keep in mind three general criteria when deciding whether to recommend the repair or restoration of any item: (1) use, (2) replaceability, and (3) value. He must further recognize that the type and extent of conservation should be based on these criteria.

Advisory Committee Chairman
Harold W. Tribolet
R. R. Donnelley & Sons Co.
Chicago, Illinois

Other Advisory Committee Members

H. Richard Archer
Williams College
Williamstown, Massachusetts

Verner W. Clapp
Council on Library Resources, Inc.
Washington, D.C.

Paul N. Banks
The Newberry Library
Chicago, Illinois

Richard W. Luce
Montana State University Library
Bozeman, Montana

Margaret C. Brown
Free Library of Philadelphia
Philadelphia, Pennsylvania

Stewart P. Smith
University of Missouri
Columbia, Missouri

Colton Storm
Sedona, Arizona

Author's Preface

The destructive effects of air pollution in the modern city upon the health of its people, its trees, and its gardens, even its buildings and statues, are well known and are being increasingly fought against [32].* But the public, generally, and even many librarians and book-collectors, who should know better, are apparently unaware of the rapid deterioration of the world's libraries under these conditions. In libraries, museums, and private homes preventive care is regularly given to pictures and sculpture, fine furniture, silver and brass; but the gradually deteriorating volumes on the shelves are given no more attention than an occasional dusting which abrades the books more than it protects them. I would judge that more than 90 per cent of the books and documents that come to my bindery for repair or restoration are in a condition that could have been avoided by regular and appropriate preventive care. Unfortunately, even when the custodians of books become aware of the problem, they may be handicapped by the relative unavailability of expert advice on what procedures to follow in conserving their libraries. The present essay is intended to meet this need.

The technical investigations upon which our knowledge of the deterioration of books is based began in the mid-nineteenth century when the growing air pollution was dramatically increased by the introduction of gas illumination in libraries. Rapid decay of some materials began to be observed, and it was noted that books were deteriorating faster in libraries using gas than in libraries that were without it, and that in gas-lit libraries books on the upper shelves were in worse condition than those on the lower shelves [6, 25]. It was also discovered at that time that books published in the nineteenth century were much more likely to show signs of decay than those published earlier. Research has subsequently shown that the book papers and leathers used prior to the first decade of the nine-

* Figures in brackets refer to items in the Selected Bibliography at the end of this pamphlet.

teenth century contained chemical ingredients that helped to counteract (though not to prevent entirely) damage by impurities in the air. Sometime after 1800 the technological advances in the printing industry created a demand for the mass production of book paper and book-covering materials. The changes made in the quality of paper and leather by mass-production methods have made these materials excessively acid, and in the pollutant-laden urban atmosphere sulphur dioxide deposited in the book materials is oxidized into the sulphuric acid which then hastens their deterioration [3, 9, 33].

As this and related processes of decay in leather and paper became known, proposals began to be made for improvements in the techniques of leather tanning [35], for the protection of materials from light [14, 17], and for the preventive treatment of bindings [33, 34]. A considerable body of scientific knowledge has begun to accumulate, and a movement is under way to establish the conservation of library materials on an equal footing with the longer established movement of conservation in the field of the fine arts.

For many years I have encouraged my clients to allow me to give their libraries of fine and rare books preventive treatment, as well as to have their most deteriorated items brought to the bindery for restoration, rebinding, or enclosure in a protective case. The reconditioning projects have ranged from the treatment of small collections of several hundred books to special collections of more than a hundred thousand books. I have used the help of my own bindery assistants for small projects and have hired and trained non-bookbinders to assist in the treatment of large libraries.

I welcome the opportunity to give a systematic account of what I have learned about organizing and conducting such library-conservation projects. However, in view of the scarcity of trained bookbinders and book-restorers, it seems only practical to approach the problem from the viewpoint of the librarian or collector, untrained in binding and restoration, and working with untrained assistants. In the following treatise I have tried to eliminate all operations requiring bookbinding skills and have suggested at appropriate points what further work, if desired, should be sent to the professional restorers.

A word of caution should be added here, however. Untrained assistants must be selected with some care. They should be neat in their work, conscientious, reasonably intelligent, and relatively skilled in working with their hands. Much damage, some of it perhaps irreparable, can be done by clumsy, careless, or inattentive help. Close supervision by the librarian or collector is desirable. In general, it should be emphasized that the repair or restoration of very rare or extremely valuable materials is best left to the professional restorer.

I wish to express appreciation to my fellow binders, Harold W. Tribolet, manager of the Department of Extra Binding, R. R. Donnelley & Sons Company, The Lakeside Press, Chicago; to Paul N. Banks, hand binder and conservator of the Newberry Library, Chicago; to Nancy and Colton Storm, hand binders of Sedona, Arizona; to H. Richard Archer, curator of the Chapin Collection at Williams College; to Margaret C. Brown, chief of the Processing Division of the Free Library, Philadelphia; to Stewart P. Smith, head of the Serials Department at the University of Missouri; and to Richard W. Luce, former assistant director of the Library Technology Program of the American Library Association, Chicago, for their patient page-by-page reading and creative criticism of the manuscript. Thanks are also due to Forrest F. Carhart, Jr., director of the Library Technology Program, for his advice and assistance, and to Herbert L. Hanna, Technical Editor of the Library Technology Program, for his special help with this second edition. I also want to thank the Council on Library Resources, Incorporated, for providing the funds that have made this effort possible. Special thanks are due to my bindery assistants, Nancy Clark, Maggy Magerstadt Fisher, Gladys Rieser, and Joel Mason, for their help in editing and proofreading the material. I also wish to thank my colleague, Laura S. Young, president of the Guild of Book Workers, for her helpful reading of the manuscript.

The manuscript of the first edition of this manual was completed before the flood in Florence on November 4, 1966. The author, as well as Harold Tribolet and Paul Banks, participated in the rescue operations, which managed to save over a million and a half flood-damaged books from destruction. During these operations we had a priceless opportunity to work with library conservators from other countries and to exchange ideas and techniques.

The outstanding figure in the organization of the rescue work at the Biblioteca Nazionale Centrale was the English binder and conservator Peter Waters. The author wishes to thank Mr. Waters for taking time from a very busy work schedule to read the first edition critically. Many of his suggestions have been incorporated into the present edition.

Last of all I owe a debt of gratitude to my daughter, Lucy, and to my husband for their editorial assistance and for their patience while this work was being written.

C. H.

Preparing To Recondition a Library

This pamphlet describes a way of setting up a project for the reconditioning of a large library of books of permanent value. By selecting only those materials and techniques which apply to his own situation, however, the owner of a small collection of books will be able to adapt this manual to his own needs.

The text is divided into three parts. The first contains suggestions for setting up a suitable work area, instructions for the removal of the books from their shelves, and a discussion of the initial cleaning and examination of the books. The second part covers the sorting of books into various treatment categories and identifies conditions needing treatment. The third section describes the treatment that each identified problem should receive.

WORK AREA

Refurbishing should be done as close to the bookshelves as possible. In the past, collections often have been treated by setting up worktables in the stacks themselves. Sawhorses and a table top that was 2 × 6 feet in size were used. Work lights were set up and attached by means of an extension cord to the nearest electric outlet. Some books that needed only dusting were reshelved at once. Other books that needed preservative treatment or minor repairs were reshelved as soon as they were treated. Those books needing major repairs were listed and then reshelved, or they were removed to some other area of the library for processing. The tables and lights were moved along through the stacks until all the books had been treated.

At the present time most librarians seem to be following the policy of positioning their stacks as close together as possible. New stacks are being built with narrower aisles. It is now usually necessary to move the books to a work area elsewhere in the library. Ideally, a workroom should be large and well lighted. There should be room for several tables. The usual table height of about 30 inches is satisfactory for the techniques described in this article. The tables need not be wider than 2 or 2½ feet. They should be strong and steady to prevent books from falling and liquids from spilling. It has been found useful to attach large book ends, about 9 inches high, to each end of the table, using small C clamps to secure them more firmly. The book ends allow books to be lined up along the back half of the table. Each worktable should have excellent overhead light; or there should be general illumination in the room, and each worker should have a good work lamp. It is impossible to do good work without good light. The tables should be covered with an absorbent paper covering, such as building paper or wrapping paper. Unprinted newsprint may also be used, although it is weak and will have to be changed more often. It is important to use an absorbent material because oil or water spots are difficult to see on a non-absorbent material, such as oilcloth or plastic-coated paper. It is essential to be able to see that the work surface is clean. It is also advisable to change the covering of the worktable often to prevent soiling the books. Printed newsprint is not recommended because it camouflages oil and water spots, and the ink rubs off.

A properly adjusted stenographer's chair is ideal for this work. Otherwise a plain wooden or metal chair should be used. Chairs upholstered in cloth should not be used, since the worker may have to shift his chair with oily hands.

Rugs should be removed if possible. If not, they should be covered with a heavy-plastic dropcloth or, better yet, with the type of plastic runners used to protect carpets from damage in wet weather.

MOVING BOOKS

Books can be badly damaged when they are moved. Libraries usually move books from one place to another by placing them on the shelves of a book truck. As the truck is wheeled along, it sometimes must be pushed over a doorsill or the edge of a rug. Unless the books are firmly supported by book ends or the end of the shelf, the books may tumble off the truck and be damaged. Using a truck that has sloping troughs protects books from falling but has disadvantages. If the books are placed on their fore edges, they may be damaged even though they cannot fall off the truck. Gravity pulls the body of the book forward out of its cover, and the weight of the book may break the joints. If such a truck is the only one available, a safer way to move the books on it would be to load the truck with the spines of the books against the back shelf of the trough.

It is recommended that books be moved in the following way: Use a library book truck that has flat shelves. Secure a dozen or more corrugated cardboard cartons of such a size that two cartons will fit on each shelf. If the shelf is 36 inches long, then the cartons might measure 16 inches long, 14 inches wide, and perhaps 10 inches high. Set up the cartons and glue the bottom flaps with a strong adhesive. Do not use staples. Push the top flaps down against the inside walls. Carrying handles may be fastened to each end of the carton. Remove the wires from wooden package-carrying handles and thread rope through the wooden tube. Then punch two holes through the end and flaps of the carton, about a third of the way down from the top. (Stronger cardboard may also be added to reinforce the corrugated board.) Push the rope through these holes and tie a square knot on the outside, leaving enough slack to allow the handle to be held comfortably. Coat the knot with strong adhesive to prevent it from working loose. Several cartons will fit on the truck. They can be removed from the truck to a worktable, emptied, and the truck wheeled back to the stacks for another load.

Commercially made tote-boxes, like the ones used by supermarkets for grocery deliveries, might be good for books. They are more costly, but last indefinitely. Moving companies sometimes sell a type of tote-box that sets up securely without stapling or gluing and that can be flattened out for storage. Whatever type of carton or box is used, it is essential that the bottoms and handles be absolutely secure to prevent any type of accident [38].

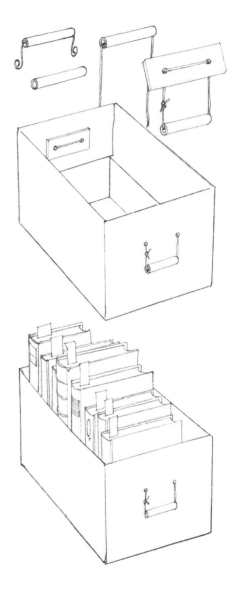

Book-carrying cartons

RECORDING THE SHELF POSITION OF BOOKS IN A CATALOGUED COLLECTION

Some thought must be given to proper record-keeping procedures before the removal of books from the shelves is begun. If the books have been catalogued, a great deal of time will be saved by recording the order in which the books are shelved. This record may be made on a chart or can be written on masking tape fastened to the bottom edge of each shelf. The record on the chart can indicate the shelf number and the span of the call numbers. Starting with the lowest call number in the room, mark the top shelf in this section Number One. The chart might read (section) 1—(shelf) 1: 913.31 to 913.33. The next notation might be (section) 1—(shelf) 2: 913.34 to 913.36 and the next (section) 1—(shelf) 3: 913.37 to 913.39. If masking tape is used on the lower edge of each shelf, the shelf and section number may be omitted; list only the span of the call numbers, that is, 913.31 to 913.33.

Even though the intent may be to move the books to a new location after treatment, it is still worthwhile to chart the original positions of the books. Such a chart indicates how many inches of shelving to allow for each category of books in a new location.

RECORDING THE SHELF POSITION OF BOOKS
IN AN UNCATALOGUED COLLECTION

If uncatalogued books are to be removed from the shelf for more than dusting, it is important to keep a record of the order of their arrangement, unless an entirely new arrangement is planned. If the books consist chiefly of sets, a sample chart may be used which reads something like this: (section) 1—(shelf) 1: Shakespeare (vols.) 1–22; (section) 1—(shelf) 2: Shakespeare (vols.) 23–28, Sterne 1–15. If the library consists of a number of cloth and leather bindings with only an occasional set, assign a number to each volume. A slip of paper, called a flag, is placed in each book. These flags should be made of acid-free lightweight Bristol board or a comparable material. A useful size is about ten inches by five-eighths of an inch. The flags are numbered consecutively. When the first shelf of books has been vacuumed and removed from the shelf, and hand-dusted as described below, immediately open the book and place a flag in the center of each volume with about an inch of paper extending above the tops of the pages. On a chart, a record is made listing what book numbers belong on each shelf. A masking-tape strip along the shelf bottom may also be useful. The chart might read: (section) 1—(shelf) 1: 1–28; 1–2: 29–54, etc. The shelf label would give only the book numbers. The time spent in making and inserting these flags is more than regained by being able to replace those books needing little or no work on the correct shelf. At the end it is a simple matter to arrange the books in numerical order and pull the flags out carefully.

VACUUMING BOOKS ON THE SHELF

Examine a sample volume from the top shelf of the first section to be treated. If the tops of the books have a significant layer of dust, then consider whether some of this might be removed while the books are still on the shelf. A tank-style vacuum cleaner is a great help in keeping the dust from being redistributed throughout the room and back onto the books. The round dusting brush that has a metal base can usually be taken apart. A piece of window screen or cheesecloth can be cut and inserted so that it covers the opening. Then the tool can be reassembled. This is now a dusting tool which will remove dust but will not suck in any loose parts of the binding. When using such a dusting tool, it is important to examine the face of the tool often; first, to retrieve any parts of the bindings which may have been picked up, and, second, to remove any accumulation of dust which might interfere with cleaning. Usually such a dusting tool can be run gently over the spines, or any exposed area, and the tops of all but the tallest books on the shelf. This will remove a large percentage of the dirt. When you are ready to remove books from the shelf after the initial vacuuming, move the book truck close to the bookshelf. Place a book carton on the truck. Fasten a towel to the end of the book truck. One end of the towel should be damp, the other dry. This will enable the worker to wipe his hands clean as often as necessary to prevent leaving finger marks on the sides of the books.

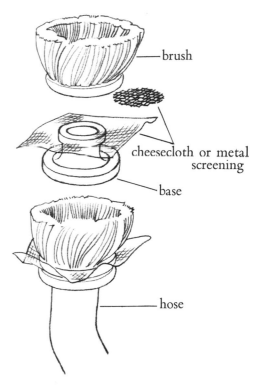

Vacuum cleaner dusting tool with protective screen

REMOVING BOOKS FROM THE SHELF

Books must never be removed from shelves by pulling at the head-caps. A safe way to begin removing books from a full shelf is to push a few books toward the back of the shelf on either side of one or two books, leaving these books free to be grasped on each side with one hand and removed from the shelf. It is now easy to remove the rest of the books by grasping as many as can be lifted safely with one hand, using the other hand to support the adjacent books. Unless one has a very strong grip, it is safer to remove only two books at a time while supporting the adjacent books with the other hand. By this method, there is a firm grip on each book being removed. Otherwise, if more than two books are being moved, those in the

REMOVING BOOKS FROM SHELF

Push adjacent books back

*Grasp the exposed books
with left hand*

*Support remaining books
with right hand*

*Lay some books on their sides
to act as support*

middle may slip and fall. If one is interrupted before a whole shelf of books has been removed, it is important to lay a few books flat to prevent those that remain from tumbling to the floor. Hands should be kept clean as work proceeds to be sure that no finger marks are left on the books.

*Dusting the head of
a book by hand*

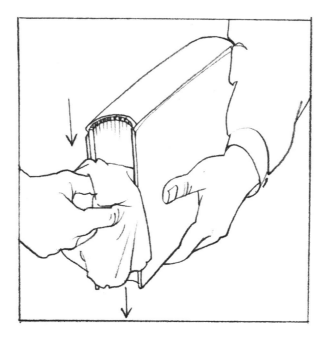

DUSTING

If the books are catalogued and a record has been made of shelf position, the books can be placed in cartons and wheeled to the workroom. Here they can be hand-dusted as they are removed from the cartons. If the books are uncatalogued and are to be flagged, it is advisable to hand-dust each book as it is removed from the shelf. Then flags should be inserted in the center of each book to indicate the order in which it was shelved.

In hand-dusting books, it is advisable to use treated cloths that help keep dust from scattering. One satisfactory brand of treated dustcloth is One-Wipe⊕.* The cloth can be hand-washed a number of times and still retain its effectiveness. Another product, Endust⊕, is a pressurized spray which can be applied to any soft cloth to turn it into an effective treated dustcloth. Both these products have been tested and do not leave harmful residues on the books. When dusting books by hand, pick up one book at a time, holding it firmly closed. Tip the head forward and slant it down, with the spine facing up. Dust the top of the pages thoroughly, stroking toward the fore edge. The book is tipped forward in this way to

* See "Supplies and Equipment," pp. 56–59, for all items carrying the symbol ⊕.

prevent dust from dropping between pages. Now dust all the other surfaces of the binding. Even after vacuuming, a considerable amount of dirt will still be removed by the treated dustcloth.

The United States National Archives moves the books to a dusting unit where a compressed air blower with a pressure of thirty to forty pounds per square inch is used to remove dust from the books. The dust is then drawn out of the room by suction [30, 38].

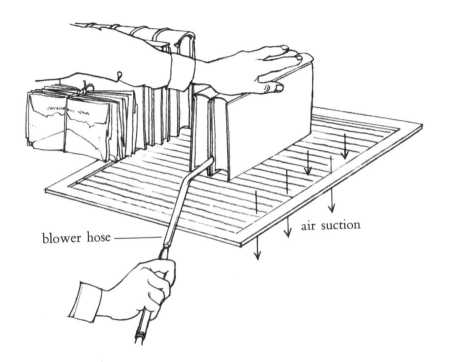

Dusting with compressed air

Sorting Books and Identifying Problems

LABELS

Now wheel the truckload of books into the work area. If the books were hand-dusted as they were put into cartons, they can be sorted immediately. If not, they should be hand-dusted as they are removed from the cartons. The well-equipped work area should have several

Heavy labels used to identify treatment

tables. If this is not possible, perhaps empty shelves will be available. Or, as a last resort, the various categories of problems can be sorted into cartons. Have labels on hand made of oblong pieces of heavy cardboard inscribed with a marking pen. Since they are heavy, they are not easily blown away or mislaid. They are to be placed on top, or in front of, stacks or cartons of books to indicate the treatment the books shall receive. Typically, a label reads "OIL," "REPAIR CORNERS," or "OPEN PAGES."

BOOK JACKETS

A general decision should be made by the curator or owner about book jackets, before treatment of a collection is begun. Jackets are very often printed on impermanent and weak paper. Evidence of acid migration from the turned-in flaps of the jacket will sometimes be observed on the end papers. Jackets tear and soil easily, and yet some bear information not included in the book. One simple solution to the problem is to remove the jackets, write the call numbers, if any, on each, and put them aside. An important book jacket might be deacidified, a process that will be discussed in another pamphlet in this series. It could then be used as a book protector. There is no doubt that a book left in an acid-free wrapper on the shelf remains cleaner than a book that is not jacketed. This same cleanliness can be achieved more safely, however, by applying a Mylar wrapper⊕ to any kind of binding.

SHARP METAL FITTINGS

Before starting to furbish a library, a decision should be made about what to do with books that have metal clasps and bosses. These often damage adjacent books, and they should not be replaced on the shelf without some form of treatment. The best treatment, of course, is to have protective containers made for such books. All books needing this treatment could be put aside under a label reading BOX. A less satisfactory treatment is to slip binder's board or felt pads between the books that have protruding bosses or clasps. Such dividers should be considered only a temporary solution to the problem, since they are likely to be displaced.

LARGE BOOKS

Felt pads give good protection when used between very large books, if these volumes are to be stacked on top of one another. Considerable damage can be done by pulling a heavy book out over a delicate binding. Ideally, each book that is to be stored flat should have its own shelf. If this is not possible, felt pads between each book will give some protection. A protective container is, however, always best.

UNTITLED SLIPCASES

When a book has been stored in an untitled slipcase and either the book or the case needs treatment, they must be separated. It is important to make a record of the title of the book that belongs in the slipcase. The title, call number, or flag number may be written on a sheet of paper which may then be crumpled and stuffed inside the slipcase. It can be a very time-consuming task to try to bring the book and slipcase together again without such a record.

LEATHER BINDINGS

All leather bindings (except for alum-tawed leather [see below]) should be put aside for possible cleaning and for treatment with preservatives. The reasons for using these preservatives, their formulae, and directions for applying them will be dealt with later in this pamphlet.

When separating these leather-bound books from the other bindings, one may come upon artificial leather that is difficult to distinguish from real leather. This leather substitute is made by pressing a plate engraved with the grain of real leather, imperfections and all, into a plastic surface. If you suspect that a covering material may be artificial leather, take it to a good light and examine wear points. These are at the turn-in of the head and tail and at the tips of the corners. Also examine the raw edge of the material where the corners are turned in. If the material is artificial leather, you may be able to detect some of the cloth threads or fiber under the coating. If you are unable to tell the difference and do apply preservatives to a book bound in artificial leather, the leather treatment proposed later in this pamphlet will do the book no serious harm. However, polishing off the oil from these bindings will be difficult, and the material may have to be cleaned with a solvent.

VELLUM AND ALUM-TAWED
LEATHER BINDINGS

Be on the lookout for books bound in vellum or alum-tawed leather. These are usually white or cream-colored, although very occasionally one will find a dyed vellum binding. Most vellum has a smooth, hard surface with almost invisible pores. Parchment, a split skin usually of sheep, is ordinarily thinner and weaker; in fact, bindings made of this material often deteriorate quite rapidly.*
Alum-tawed leather (usually referred to simply as "tawed" leather)

* Since, for the purposes of this manual, the procedures for the treatment and repair of vellum and parchment are more or less identical, we shall hereafter refer only to vellum, which should be understood to include parchment also.

is usually thicker and has a slightly less hard and shiny surface than vellum. The most commonly tawed skins are those of the pig, which have fairly conspicuous pores or hair follicles. The typical alum-tawed pigskin binding will have raised bands, the skin having originally been pliable enough to be stretched. This material was most frequently used between the twelfth and sixteenth centuries. Put books bound in these materials aside, segregated from the other leather bindings. If there are enough of them in the collection, they can be stacked separately. Otherwise, they can be kept with the cloth and paper bindings, as many of their problems are the same.

INSPECTING CLOTH, PAPER, TAWED LEATHER, AND VELLUM BINDINGS

Having put all non-tawed leather bindings aside, you can concentrate on inspecting the cloth, paper, tawed leather, and vellum bindings. As you spot each problem, you should put the problem book near or under the appropriate label.

BOOKPLATES

If bookplates are to be inserted in the books, the time to mount the plates is when all the books are off the shelf. This can be done right after they are brought into the workroom and before they are sorted into their various treatment categories. However, bookplates should not be mounted in leather bindings until after treatment, when the hinges will be more flexible. If the books are very dirty, bookplating may be postponed until after cleaning.

ENCLOSURES

Carefully flip through the leaves of the cloth, paper, vellum, and tawed leather bindings, looking for enclosures in each book. Some enclosures will be found which are clearly accidental, such as scraps of paper inserted as bookmarks. These scraps are often made of acid paper and will sometimes be found to have marked the pages. Usually they can be discarded at once. Look for and remove pins, paper clips, and rubber bands. Any mark that they may have made will be most difficult to remove without taking the book apart. It is best to make a note of the damage and to have the damage examined by an expert. Some other kinds of enclosures that will be found are newspaper and magazine clippings, usually stories about the author or reviews of the book; such parts of the book jacket as a biography or picture of the author; or letters from the author. Books with these pertinent enclosures should be put aside under the ENCLOSURE label.

ACID MIGRATION

While examining books, be alert for other kinds of acid migration. These can come not only from enclosures but from acid parts of the book itself. One condition is the presence of so-called protective tissues over the illustrations. These were put into the book to prevent the ink used for printing the illustrations from offsetting onto the pages. These tissues may have turned brown because of acid content,

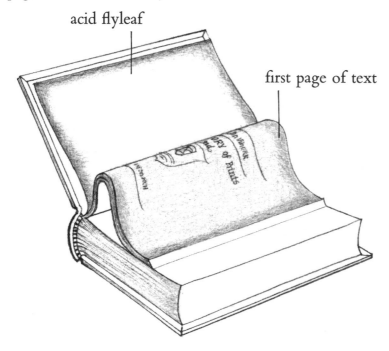

acid flyleaf

first page of text

Checking for acid migration from end papers to text pages

transferring this acid to the illustration and to the opposite leaves. Also be on the lookout for illustrations that have developed the freckle-like spots known as "foxing" and that are staining adjacent leaves. Acid binder's board may also be found. Certain nineteenth-century cloth bindings seem to be afflicted with this condition. A brown stain will be observed to have traveled through the board paper. Wherever the cloth was turned over the inside of the board, the end paper will not be stained, since the cloth has acted as a barrier to acid migration. Sometimes the acid will have affected several leaves. Some end papers are made of highly acid stock which often has become discolored. The discoloration in turn migrates to the first and last leaves of the text of the book in many instances. Sometimes one can see the end papers turning yellow along the three margins that are exposed to the air. If you arch back the first leaf or so of the book and find that the leaf nearest the acid end paper is definitely changing color in comparison to subsequent leaves, you should set this book aside for treatment. Folded maps are sometimes inserted in pockets in the back of the book. Pull these out and examine them. Sometimes the pocket is made of a cut in the end papers, and the map is held between the end paper and the board. Thus it is partly in contact with the binder's board underneath. If a brown stain appears on part of the map, put this book aside for treatment. Another form of discoloration is the stain on the first flyleaf caused by the turn-in of a leather cover or by leather bookplates. Such stains often travel through several pages. Since steps can be taken to prevent this, books with this problem should also be put aside on the ACID MIGRATION pile.

LEAF REPAIR AND LOOSE PLATES

Check through the books looking for old repairs. Some of these may have been made with pressure-sensitive plastic tape, and books containing such repairs must be set aside for treatment. Some kinds of pressure-sensitive plastic tape leave a stubborn brown stain after even a short period of time. Other kinds begin to ooze at the edges and eventually cause leaves to stick together. Tender old paper has a tendency to break at the edges of the tape. All these tapes should be removed.

The one safe prepared tape to use for repair is Dennison's Transparent Mending Tape⊕, made of glassine paper backed with a water-soluble adhesive. Although the glassine paper eventually turns yellow, it will not stain the repaired leaf itself. A repair made with this material need not be removed.

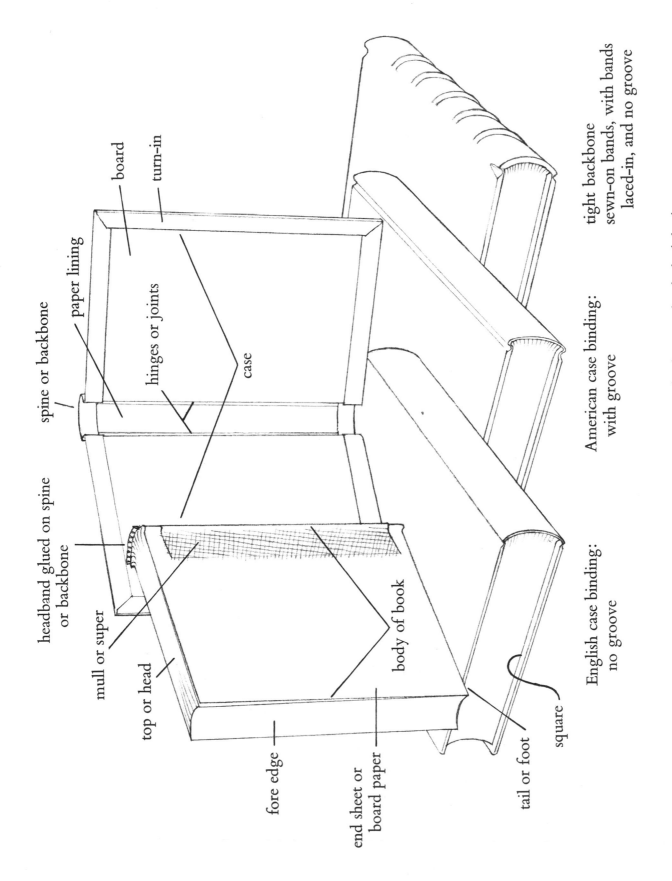

spine or backbone

paper lining

board

turn-in

hinges or joints

case

headband glued on spine or backbone

mull or super

top or head

fore edge

end sheet or board paper

body of book

tail or foot

square

tight backbone sewn-on bands, with bands laced-in, and no groove

American case binding: with groove

English case binding: no groove

Construction of English and American case bindings, and tight-back book

15

Be on the lookout for torn leaves. It is common to find that the hinges of folded maps or charts have begun to tear. Look for loose illustrations.

Keep a container of colored strips of paper (flags) and, as torn leaves or plastic-tape repairs, etc., are discovered, slip one into the book to indicate where each repair is needed. These flags can be color-coded, the colors indicating whether an old repair is to be removed or a new tear is to be repaired. Later on, when you are ready to start repair, it will save time not to have to search for the problem leaf.

TIGHTENING BOOKS IN THEIR CASES

As case bindings are examined, watch for books that are loose in their cases. This condition is very common and can be observed even in books that have never been used or in new books fresh from the publisher. In the manufacture of case bindings, the pages are sewed or secured with an adhesive; a fold of end paper is tipped on front and back, the spine is glued, the edges trimmed and perhaps gilded or colored; the book is rounded and backed and the spine lined with super and a heavy paper lining. Meanwhile, the case is made separately and titled. When both the body of the book and the case are ready, the two parts are brought together. This operation is called "casing-in."

Sometimes a book has not been properly attached in its case. The body of the book will then drag forward and the bottoms of the leaves will touch the shelf. The upper part of the spine will cave in and the end papers will begin to work loose. Eventually these may break at the hinge area so that the super, which lines the spine and which comes out an inch or so over the sides of the book, will be the only thing holding the book in its case. When the super breaks, the book will need recasing or rebinding, and cannot be properly repaired except by a professional binder.

In order to see which books need tightening in their cases, proceed as follows: Lay a book on the worktable. Raise the front cover and suspend it at a right angle to the book. With your right index finger placed just above the inside hinge of the end paper, push the cover as if to push it open, but continue to hold the board perpendicular with the left hand so that the board cannot open out flat. If the book is loose in its case, you will see the spine of the case move away from the backbone of the book and a loose area will appear in the joint under the end paper. Books with this problem should be put aside under a label marked TIGHTEN.

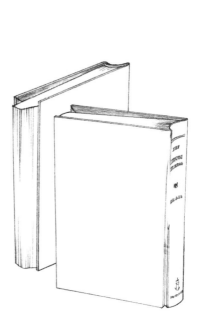

Books loose in their cases

*Identifying books
that are loose in their cases*

CLEAN INSIDE

As you examine books, look for signs of dust that may have sifted down between the pages. This will be found most often where the leaves are rippled, or the boards warped, or the top of the book un-trimmed. Vellum books are more likely to be warped than others, so pay particular attention to them. Sometimes dust is found between the end papers, sometimes throughout the entire book. Where a folded map or chart occurs in a book, an opening is often formed that allows dust to sift down between the leaves. Put such books under a CLEAN INSIDE label. Flags should be inserted to indicate the positions of the dusty pages.

CLEAN TOPS

The advantage of having the tops of books gilded becomes apparent when any library is inspected. The gold "seals" the top edges so that dust does not sift down between the pages. Thus they are more easily cleaned. Examine the tops of ungilded books. Many may be quite soiled. Put these aside for special cleaning under a label marked CLEAN TOPS.

OPEN LEAVES

Books are sometimes bound with the leaves untrimmed and the original folds intact. A policy decision should be made by the curator or owner about such unopened leaves or bolts. In any library where the books are allowed to circulate, we recommend that the bolts be opened properly before the books are shelved. Otherwise readers may attempt to open the leaves with a pencil or the fingers and damage the book. Put books with unopened leaves aside under a label reading OPEN LEAVES.

However, if the bolts are dusty or dirty, the books should first go to the pile marked CLEAN TOPS, to be opened later.

CLEAN OUTSIDE

Examine the outsides of the cloth, paper, tawed leather, and vellum bindings for dirt, such as finger marks or grime due to age. Put these books aside for treatment under a CLEAN OUTSIDE label.

COLOR

Sometimes the corners, board edges, head, and tail of the cloth bindings have lost their color. The appearance of books with this problem can be improved by proper recoloring. Such books should be put in the COLOR pile.

SEAL HEADS AND TAILS

Cloth bindings are subject to wear from friction. Usually the first sign of wear is fraying of the threads at the head and tail of the spine. When the coating of the cloth has rubbed off, the exposed threads fray and then begin to break. Next, the cloth at the top of the spine tears away, leaving the hinges vulnerable to being torn.

All cloth bindings should be examined for signs of fraying. When you observe these, put the book aside under the SEAL HEADS AND TAILS label.

LOOSE LABELS

Labels made of paper or leather are occasionally found on cloth, paper, tawed leather, or vellum bindings. Sometimes they are loose or have come off entirely. Put all these books under the LOOSE LABEL heading.

REBUILD CORNERS

Look for broken corners on the cloth, paper, tawed leather, and vellum books. Put these aside under the REBUILD CORNERS label.

STAPLES

When going through a pamphlet collection, you will often find that the staples have rusted and stained the pages. In some cases rust may cause the adjacent paper to disintegrate. Put these stapled pamphlets aside under the STAPLES label so that staples can be removed and the pamphlets properly sewed.

WRITE-UP

Certain books will be found that are obviously in a serious state of deterioration. (If many such books are found and they seem to be deteriorating at a fairly rapid rate, the librarian or collector should undertake a serious investigation of the conditions under which these books are being stored and used to determine what may be causing the damage.) It is important not to attempt to repair or patch such books, unless this can be done correctly. Usually these books must be sent to a professional bookbinder. Some may be candidates for simple cloth binding, while others should perhaps go to a fine binder for restoration or rebinding by hand. Such books may be put aside under the WRITE-UP label. By this we mean that a notation can be made later indicating the fact that this book needs further repair.

After inspection of all the cloth, paper, tawed leather, and vellum books that have been brought into the workroom, large numbers of them often are found to be in good condition. If the collection of books has been receiving regular care and if the library is properly air-conditioned the year round, it may well be that all the cloth, paper, tawed leather, and vellum books can be returned to the shelf with no more than a careful dusting. Other leather books will, of course, require further treatment. The reasons for treating these leather bindings regularly will be discussed later on in this pamphlet.

Treatment

We are now ready to begin the actual work of giving the books preventive treatment. Books will have been sorted into their various treatment categories. As the processes described below are completed, the books may be put aside under a label marked INSPECT. The books will be reinspected, and perhaps it will be found that some need more work. Place them in another category, under another label, for further treatment. When a book needs no further treatment, it can be put aside under a label marked SHELVE.

BOOKPLATES

Although the plating of books is not strictly a part of the reconditioning of a library, we have so consistently found it to be a part of the job that we have included a description of a technique for plating at this point. Even in a catalogued and plated collection we often find a significant number of books that have been shelved without plating. A private collector who wishes to have his collection as a whole reconditioned may decide to have his bookplates applied while the books are off the shelf being cleaned and repaired.

All paper bookplates should be made of acid-free paper. Plates should be printed with the grain of the paper running from the top to the bottom of the plate and not across it. When the adhesive is applied to the bookplate, the paper first expands across the grain and then shrinks when it dries. Sometimes this shrinking causes the book board to warp. If the grain of the bookplate paper is vertical, warping will be less pronounced than if the grain runs across the plate. The bookplate should be comparatively small, possibly 2 inches by 3 inches. A plate of this size will fit the smallest book regularly shelved in most collections, since books under 3 inches in height are usually classified as miniatures. Institutions customarily place the plate just above the center on the inside of the front board if possible. If there is no room here, you may apply the plate to the back board paper.

If both board papers have printing, writing, maps, or other book-plates present, the flyleaves, either front or back, will have to be used. To avoid warping the flyleaf, the plate can be tipped in, with paste applied only to the top edge.

Private collectors might consider placing their plate at the upper-left corner inside the front cover to allow room for the plates of future owners.

If the bookplates are to be applied by hand, assemble the following materials: a piece of heavy glass or a lithographic stone about 12 × 14 inches in size, a paste brush⊕ some 2 inches in diameter or a flat brush 2 or 3 inches wide, unprinted newsprint sheets or unsized yellow second sheets (called manila), a rubber brayer of the kind used for inking in linoleum-block printing⊕, a sharp knife or scalpel, waxed paper, and paste.

The paste should be one that is pure and that will not stain the bookplate or end paper. We use a prepared, precooked, and dehy-drated wheat paste sold by Samuel Schweitzer Co. as Wheat Paste No. 6⊕. To mix the paste, put cold water in a paste bowl and pour the powdered paste in gradually, stirring. The correct consistency of the paste can be determined by experimentation, but we would de-scribe it to be that of mayonnaise. Start with no more than four books and four plates. Lay the four books on their back covers in a row along your worktable. Starting with the lefthand book, open out the front cover and rest it on some support, perhaps another book or a pack of yellow second sheets. Now go down the line from left to right, opening each front cover and laying it on the first flyleaf of the previous volume.

Having dipped your brush in the paste bowl, wipe off any excess. Cover the surface of the glass or stone smoothly with paste, going over it several times with the brush. The amount of paste on the stone or glass should be such that in running the index finger down the surface, no very clearly defined trough is made. One learns from practice what the thickness of the paste should be, as well as how heavily to apply it to the stone or glass. Pick up the first bookplate and lay it down right side up on the pasted surface. When all four bookplates have been laid out in this way, cover the whole surface of the glass or stone with wastepaper and roll the rubber brayer over

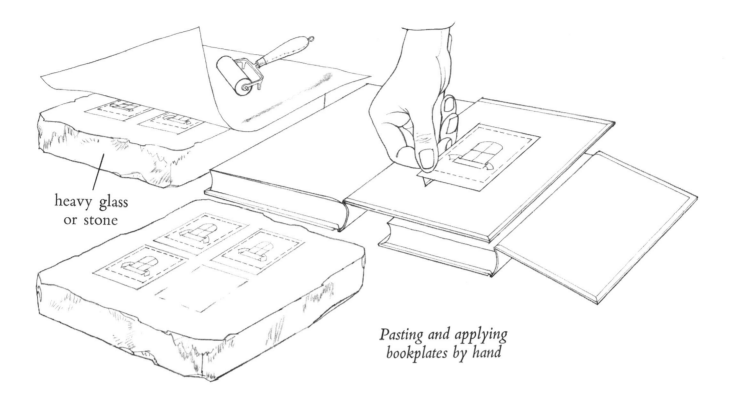

*Pasting and applying
bookplates by hand*

it. Lift up the waste sheet and throw it away. You will now have all four bookplates lying on a comparatively clean stone with all the paste on one side of the bookplate and none on the other. If paste has oozed out onto the bookplate, the paste was laid on the glass or stone too thickly; use less paste next time and brush it on thinner. Now, taking the scalpel or knife, lift up the corner of the first bookplate with its tip. This facilitates grasping the corners neatly. Bring it over to the first board cover and lay it in position as squarely as possible. Place a sheet of wastepaper over the plate and roll the brayer over it. Discard the waste sheet. Proceed to lay the remaining bookplates in position and rub them down. If, when you reach the last plate, the paste has dried out and the paper sticks to the stone, you should paste up fewer plates next time until you begin to acquire speed. Eventually, you should be able to paste at least eight bookplates at once. If possible, allow room on the table so that the first row of books can be pushed to the back to air-dry. Even so, when you are ready to close the book, it is a good idea to place a fold of waxed paper between the board cover and the end paper to prevent moisture from traveling into the book.

Leather bookplates should be sprayed with some product such as Krylon No. 1301⊕ to prevent the acid transfer onto the first flyleaf that will occur from contact with the leather. The plates should be sprayed before they are mounted. They should be applied with an adhesive that moistens the leather as little as possible. Wetting, which stretches the leather, causes raising of the impression of the stamping and, often, loosening of the gold. We use a less watery adhesive such as Jade No. 454⊕ for this. The leather plates must be pasted one at a time and applied to the board paper at once, since the adhesive is absorbed very quickly by the leather.

Bookplates may be applied more efficiently with the aid of a bookplate pasting or gluing machine⊕.

ENCLOSURES

All enclosures that have been identified as not pertinent to the book, such as scraps of paper, paper clips, or pressed flowers, should be removed. Certain pertinent enclosures will be found that either may be so bulky as to put a strain on the joints of the books, or may open up the pages of the books sufficiently to let dust seep in. Other enclosures made of acid paper, such as modern newsprint, may have left a stain on the book pages. Such items may be put in acid-free envelopes on which the title or call number of the book is written. If modern newspaper clippings and other materials on poor paper are to be kept, they should be sent out to be deacidified and laminated with cellulose acetate. This treatment will be discussed in a later pamphlet.

In a private collection or rare-book room, letters from the author, unless very bulky, are usually kept with the book. They may be hinged on the leaf following the first flyleaf. There they will cause less strain on the joints of the binding than if they were laid in, or hinged in, on the first flyleaf. When hinging a letter into a book, use a strip of strong hinge paper (Japanese papers such as Shizuoka⊕ or Sekishu⊕ are ideal), clean wastepaper, wheat paste, a brush, and waxed paper. The hinge paper should be about three-eighths of an inch wide and the length of the letter. A three-sixteenths-of-an-inch strip of paste should be applied to the under part of the letter. To apply the paste, place the letter face down on a piece of clean wastepaper. Lay a second piece of wastepaper three-sixteenths of an inch

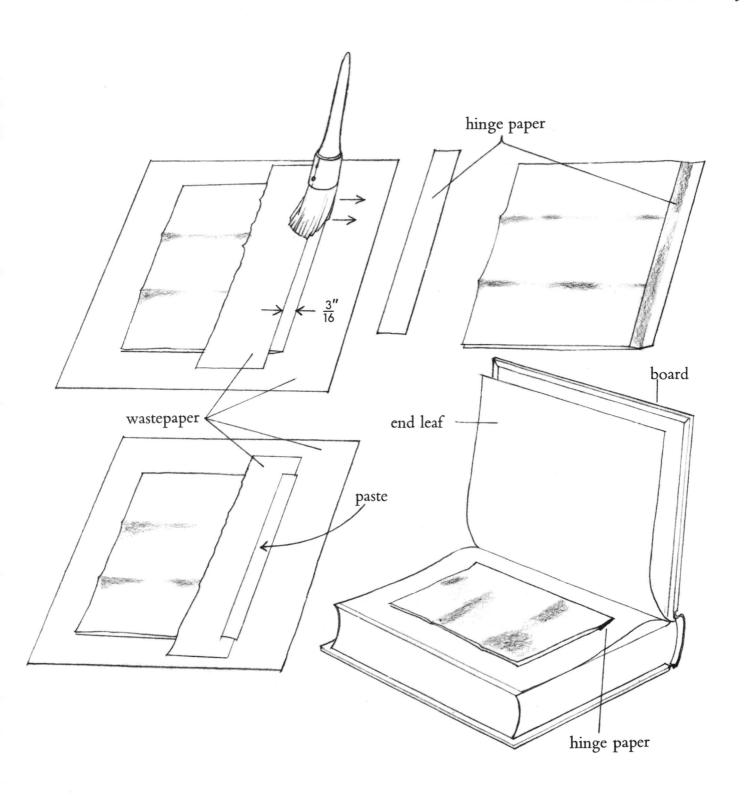

Hinging a letter into a book

from the back edge of the letter. Then apply the paste, always brushing it out onto the wastepaper in order not to drag or force paste under the letter. Remove and discard the waste sheet. The letter is then moved to a clean piece of wastepaper and the hinge strip is laid on over the paste, with half the strip extending beyond the edge of the letter. The strip is patted down onto the letter and the whole allowed to air-dry. When dry, the hinge should be folded back on itself, a strip of wastepaper slipped under it, and paste applied. Remove the wastepaper and lay the letter in position on the second flyleaf, slightly above the center of the page with the margins even. Slide a piece of waxed paper under the letter and over that part of the hinge strip that is pasted to the page. Another sheet of waxed paper may be laid over the letter, the board closed, and a weight—such as a wrapped brick—laid on top of the book until the repair has dried.

A better treatment for a valuable book would be to have a protective container with acid-free linings made for both book and letter. Then the letter may be tipped in on one of the flyleaves; or it may be placed in a folder and put into the protective container along with the book, where it cannot damage the book in any way.

ACID MIGRATION

When protective tissues that bear no printing turn brown and transfer stain to the illustration and the leaves of the book, they should be removed and discarded. The ink of the illustration has long since dried and continuing offset is rarely found. After a year or so the tissues have usually outlived their usefulness.

If the tissue is turning brown but has the title of the illustration printed on it, the only solution is to add loose barrier sheets on either side of the tissue. A sheet of paper slightly smaller than the leaf of the book will be effective. The barrier sheets should always be made of sized paper; unsized paper may let the stain travel through to the next leaf.

Where acid binder's board under the end papers is causing staining, a heavier-weight barrier sheet should be placed between the board paper and the first flyleaf. If the end paper is acid, place a barrier sheet after the first flyleaf. A folded map that shows stain from partial contact with the binder's board should be wrapped in a folder of well-sized paper and replaced in the pocket. To stop the staining on the first flyleaf caused by the turn-in of a leather cover or to prevent a leather bookplate from staining the flyleaf, place a loose barrier sheet between the board and the first flyleaf.

LEAF REPAIR AND LOOSE PLATES

All pressure-sensitive plastic mending tape should be removed. Any one of a number of solvents will dissolve the adhesive behind the tape. It may be difficult, however, to find a solvent that will not affect the printing ink. Start with a mixture of equal parts of toluene and hexane, as recommended by the U.S. National Archives [31]. Acetone actually dissolves not only the adhesive but also the plastic tape. This makes it a useful solvent when the back of the tape is inaccessible, but it also is more likely to dissolve printer's ink than some of the other solvents. Test the effect of the solvent on the ink first. Dip a cotton swab in the solvent and rub the solvent lightly over a period or comma. If the ink is not affected, try to dissolve the adhesive of the tape by applying the solvent to the reverse side of the leaf. Where the plastic tape has been applied to both sides of the leaf, it will be necessary to work the solvent in under the tape and gradually lift it as the adhesive softens. Great care should be taken not to lift the printing off the page. Should this happen inadvertently, save the piece of tape that contains the printing. After the rest of the tape has been removed, apply flour paste to the film of printing on the tape and to the spot on the page from which it came; fit the two together as exactly as possible and let dry under light pressure. Then proceed to remove the plastic tape by applying solvent to the back of the leaf. Since all organic solvents are fire and health hazards, the work should be done in a well-ventilated room, away from open flames.

When the tape has been removed, the original tear will be revealed. This damage should now be repaired. A quick, safe method of repair is to use Dennison's Transparent Mending Tape⊕.* This glassine paper tape with a water-soluble adhesive backing has been in use for more than fifty years. Although the glassine paper eventu-

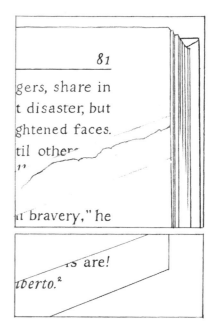

Replacing text accidentally removed from page by plastic tape

---

* If the tape is to be applied to a very thin paper, it is usually a good idea to serrate the edges of the tape with pinking shears. This will reduce the possibility of wrinkling the paper and will also eliminate the hard edges of the tape, which sometimes tend to break when placed under stress.

ally turns yellow and the tape may come loose, we have never seen or heard of an instance of this product staining the page to which it is attached.

A more professional method of preparing torn leaves involves the use of paste and Green's 105 Lens Tissue⊕. Cut or tear strips of the tissue to approximately the shape required to cover the tear. Apply thin paste to the torn area, being sure to apply paste between both overlapping edges of the tear. Lay the tissue down over the paste. The pasted area should extend no more than $\frac{1}{8}$ inch beyond the tear. Press the tissue down onto the pasted area with a piece of facial tissue. Pull or tease off any tissue beyond the pasted area, leaving tissue fibers over the torn area. Finally, blot off any excess paste.

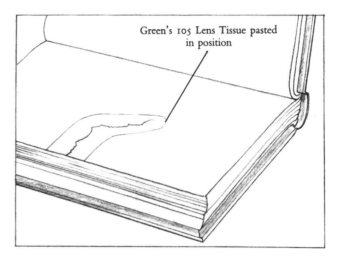

Repairing a leaf

Tissue repairs need not be applied to both sides of the sheet. In the case of edge tears, the major repair may be on the verso, but a small amount of the tissue may be brought over the edge onto the recto.

Torn folded maps will often be found. If the map is hinged into the book, the lower edge of the hinge area is particularly vulnerable. It is a tricky thing to open out and repair a torn map and have the image match. As soon as the paste strikes the paper the water in the paste causes the paper to expand. Now the two parts of the map no longer line up. The amateur would be better advised to make a temporary repair with Dennison's Transparent Mending Tape. Do not use pressure-sensitive tape of any kind for the repair of torn paper or for the consolidation of loose parts of a binding. For a permanent repair, we suggest putting such a book in the WRITE-UP pile for future treatment by a professional.

When loose plates are found in a book, study the structure to see how the plates were originally attached to the book. Usually, in an edition binding, the plates have been tipped onto the text pages. In a hand-bound book the binder may have hinged the plate into the book. You may replace a loose plate by hinging it in, following the technique described above for attaching letters from authors into the book. Sometimes, however, the addition of the hinge paper will add enough thickness at the area of the spine to cause a dangerous strain on the joints of the binding. In this case, the illustration should be tipped back into position, using the following technique for attaching a plate into a book. Check first to be sure where the plate belongs. Then place the plate face down on a piece of clean wastepaper. Place another piece of wastepaper over the verso of the plate, leaving about one-eighth of an inch of the gutter edge exposed. Brush paste over this exposed area. Remove the covering sheet, lift up the plate, and insert it into position in the book. Close the book, checking the correctness of the plate's position. Slip in waxed paper on each side to prevent any accidental damage from a stray spot of paste, or from paste oozing at the back edge. The piece of waxed paper covering the recto should be inserted all the way into the gutter, while that on the verso of the plate is placed about one-eighth of an inch out from the gutter. Place a light weight on the book. A wrapped brick makes a good weight for this purpose.

TIGHTENING BOOKS IN THEIR CASES

All those edition bindings found to be loose in their cases should be carefully examined. Some of these cased-in books may have deteriorated too far to be saved. If the hinges of the end papers are broken, the repair can still be made, but it will not be as neat as if the problem had been treated earlier. If, however, the super has torn, the book should be put aside for professional rebinding or restoration.

To prepare to tighten books in their cases, assemble the following: a bottle of polyvinyl acetate emulsion adhesive such as Jade No. 403$^{\oplus}$, stored in a bottle with a narrow opening such as the one shown in the illustration, a thin knitting needle (approximately

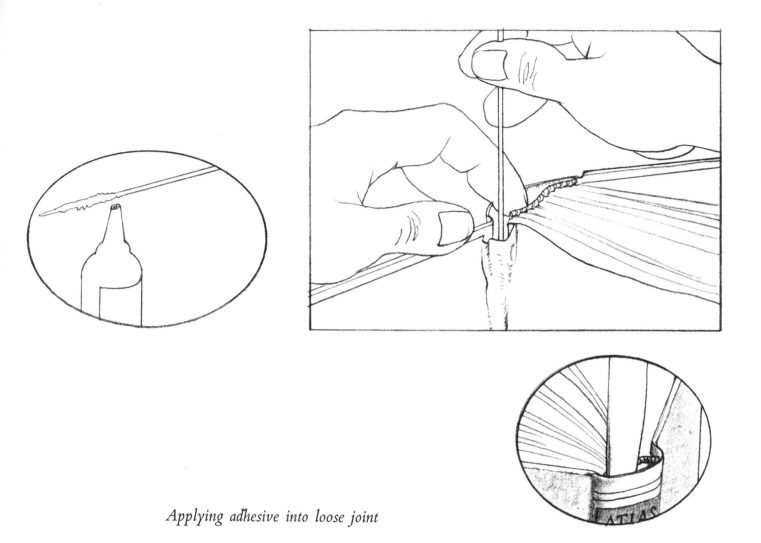

Applying adhesive into loose joint

No. 3), waxed paper, a combination press⊕ [21] such as the one shown on page 31 (or brass-bound pressing boards and a press, preferably a standing one), and a bone folder⊕. Stand the book upright. Place the tip of your left index finger into the space between the back of the pages and the spine of the case if possible. If not, push the board back to reveal the unpasted area under the end paper near the joint. Dip the knitting needle into the bottle of adhesive. When you withdraw the needle, if the opening is narrow enough, just the right amount of adhesive will cling to the needle. Push the adhesive-coated needle down into the space at the hinge area and as far back under the end paper as it will reach. Keep all parts of the spine and case free of adhesive. When you have applied adhesive to the front and back hinge areas from the top and bottom of the book, slip waxed paper between the end papers all the way into the back fold. Slide the book into the combination press until the overhanging

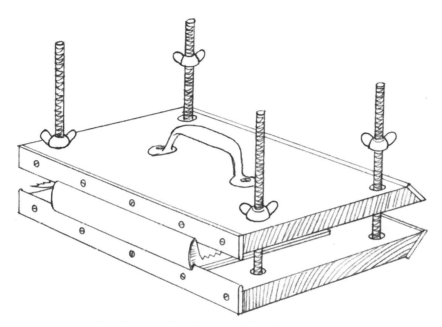

Tightening book in combination press

brass edges are fitted down into the grooves of the book at the joint area. Tighten the front screws of the press just enough to give a firm pressure. Tighten them evenly; excessive or uneven tightening might cut the cloth. If the book that needs tightening is an English case binding without a groove, do not attempt to press a groove into the cloth, as this may cut the joint. Rather, apply the adhesive under the end paper, as described above, insert the waxed paper, and press the book in the combination press, using the pressing edges that do not have overhanging brass flanges.

When the second book has been pasted, the first may be removed from the press. Open it to see whether adhesive has oozed out. If so, remove the adhesive before it dries and lay the book on its side for an hour or two, leaving the waxed papers in position. After tightening a dozen or so, examine the first books treated. Open each book in the middle and examine the cloth spine. Does it open freely, or has some adhesive oozed out and caused the spine strip of the case to stick to the backbone of the book? If the latter is the case, take a long bone folder with a rounded end, work it into the hollow of the spine area, and loosen the spine strip from the backbone of the book. Leave the book open to air-dry for a short time.

To avoid waste motion in tightening and loosening the press, arrange books that need tightening according to their thickness. Start with the thickest one and end with the thinnest.

CLEAN INSIDE

The first step in cleaning the inside of a book is to wipe the pages with a new, clean, treated dustcloth. This will remove a great deal of dirt. If there is still more dust to be removed, try wallpaper cleaner. One brand, Absorene⊕, has been tested and found to be harmless to the materials in books. Knead the Absorene to remove any crust that may have formed on the outside. If the Absorene seems sticky, allow it to dry in the air for several hours or days. When it is no longer sticky, keep it in an airtight container. If it begins to dry out too much, sprinkle it with a little water and return it to an airtight container. By the next day the moisture will have been evenly absorbed. A handful of this cleaner will remove dust from a large area quickly without affecting pencil notations or printing ink. The cleaning motion should be from the center toward the edges. To clean the edges, hold the paper firmly with the hand to avoid tearing it.

It is important when using this product to work on a separate table and to have only the book being treated on the table. The crumbs of this product tend to accumulate unless one is careful. If a crumb is left in a book or a book is set down on a crumb, the crumb will dry and adhere to whatever it touches. Fortunately, a spot of water on the crumb will cause it to loosen up and it can be removed without harm. If a crumb should be left in a book, tests have shown that it will not have a harmful effect, except for the danger of causing pages to stick together.

Another tested product is called Opaline⊕ cleaner. This is a cloth bag containing absorbent powder and other ingredients. It can be

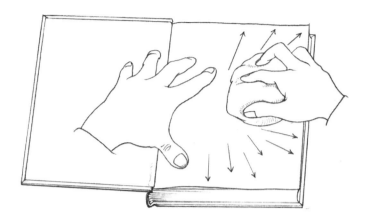

Cleaning a page with wallpaper cleaner

used to remove dirt from illustrations or pages without any danger of affecting the ink. It is also safe for use on fragile paper.

Stubborn dirt spots may be removed with an eraser. Two effective brands, Pink Pearl⊕ and Magic-Rub⊕, have been tested and found to leave no harmful residues. Since they both contain abrasives, they should not be used vigorously over printed areas or on certain coated papers. In erasing, the motion should be from the center out.

Stains of unknown origin that have penetrated through the leaves of the book are very difficult to remove without damaging the paper and printing. Books with such stains should be put aside in the WRITE-UP pile, and the problem leaf marked with a colored flag. A professional conservator should be consulted about removal of the stain.

CLEANING MAPS AND BROADSIDES

One very often comes across maps or broadsides that need attention. These have often been rolled or folded and usually show signs of dust. Unfold or unroll the material on a flat, clean surface that is larger than the item to be treated. Small weights covered with wrapping paper may be placed around the edges of a rolled item that tries to reroll itself. Absorene wallpaper cleaner, Opaline, or even fresh white bread without the crust will be effective in removing loose dust. The further treatment and the safe storage of maps and broadsides will be discussed in another pamphlet in this series.

In general, you should attempt to store these materials flat in a folder, portfolio, or box.

CLEAN TOPS

Some ungilded tops which have become soiled through exposure to dust respond well to brisk rubbing with absorbent cotton or the treated dustcloth. Further cleaning can be achieved by erasing the tops with either the Pink Pearl or the Magic-Rub eraser. Be sure to tip the top of the book forward as you erase so that the soiled crumbs of the eraser do not fall down between the pages. Books with uncut pages should be erased before the pages are cut. After erasing, brush off stray crumbs. Do not erase gilt tops.

OPEN LEAVES

If it has been decided that the uncut leaves of the books should be opened, check all books for this condition. It is usually, but not always, easy to determine which leaves are uncut by looking down on the tops of the leaves. To open the leaves correctly, use a long, narrow, thin knife, not too sharp, with a rounded, rather than a pointed, end. Insert the knife between the pages, holding the blade as nearly parallel to the fold as possible. Cut by pushing the knife outward rather than by sawing the fold open. Be careful not to cut folded maps and plates.

CLEAN OUTSIDE

A group of commercially prepared products designed to clean the outsides of cloth bindings has been identified and tested. The products are: Demco Book Cleaner⊕, Delkote Bookleen⊕ (both liquid and "gel" types), and Goddard's Book Restorer for Cloth Bindings⊕. None of these products leaves a harmful residue in the binding materials on which they are used. They may be used safely in attempting to remove the dirt embedded in cloth bindings.

However, we have found that, in general, the dirt on starch-filled cloth bindings does not yield easily to any of these products. Much of the dirt seems to be removed by soap or detergent and water. But the use of water, except on waterproof cloth, is not recommended, since it removes the starch sizing and color on the surface. It also

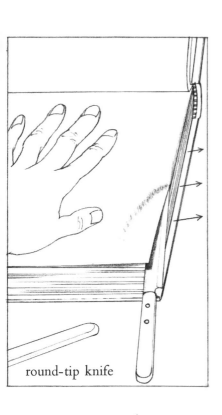

round-tip knife

How to open leaves

removes, or fills in, the gold stamping. If one attempts to wash a book, avoiding the stamped area, the difference between the cleaned and the uncleaned area is often apparent. Normally the commercial products do not damage the stamping, but they do not clean the cloth very well either. We have come to the conclusion that erasing is about as effective as any cleaning method we have tried. Erasing is especially recommended for paper and vellum bindings. The tested Pink Pearl and Magic-Rub erasers are excellent for this purpose and do not seem to affect the stamping, although care should be taken not to rub over the gold more than necessary.

Fingerprints will sometimes yield to the application of a solvent, such as hexane, on a piece of absorbent cotton. The solvent should be tested to make sure that it does not change the color of the covering material or affect the stamping.

COLOR

It has been known for a long time that sunlight has a damaging effect on various materials, causing not only fading but also general deterioration. For generations many librarians have attempted to prevent sunlight from shining on the books. Only in more recent times has research proven that artificial light is also damaging. The most harmful kind is fluorescent light. Incandescent light is also a threat, but to a lesser degree [14, 17]. The subject of lighting and of the prevention of damage to archival materials from light will be discussed fully in another pamphlet in this series.

Meanwhile, we are faced with the fact that the spines of many books on library shelves will be a different color from the sides. Almost all leather fades out to the original tan of the undyed hide. Black, dark blue, red, and tan leathers maintain their color best. Cloth bindings also fade. The question is: Should an attempt be made to restore the color to these faded spines? We strongly advise against any such attempt. It requires great skill to recolor faded spines without disfiguring the stamping, especially by obscuring it with color when attempting to color around it. Under no circumstances should one color the folds of the sections exposed by a torn or incomplete spine in an attempt to disguise the damage. For one thing, there is a danger of the color penetrating into the gutter margins of the leaves and staining the inside pages of the book. Color touch-ups should be confined to areas such as worn heads and tails, scuffed edges, and broken corners.

If you attempt to recolor these areas, it is important to choose a safe coloring agent. Colored ink is definitely not safe. Some of the chemicals in ink are harmful to leather and may also have a damaging effect on cloth. Dr. Martin's Synchromatic Transparent Water Colors⊕ are known to be safe. These are available in liquid form and in many colors. They may be mixed with each other and diluted if necessary. In order to avoid the danger of spilling, we keep the bottles upright in a waterproof container, such as a shallow plastic refrigerator container. The bottles, wedged in with filler to prevent them from tipping over, should be kept in this container while they are uncapped.

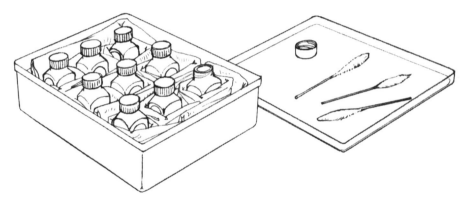

Water colors and swabs safely placed at work area

The colors may be applied to the books with a cotton swab. Have a separate swab for each color. The used swabs should be kept on a small tray, such as the top of the refrigerator container, to avoid the danger of putting the book down on one while the color is still wet.

SEAL HEADS AND TAILS

Cloth books have been put aside in a separate category when the fabric at the head and tail is fraying. Sometimes threads that have lost both their sizing and their color will look white. The appearance of such books may be greatly improved by the following treatment. First, touch up the cloth with Dr. Martin's Synchromatic Water Colors. Test the color you plan to use first, remembering that water color is darker when it is wet. The color may need to be grayed or altered in order to blend into the old binding color. A knowledge of color mixing is essential. If the worker has had no training in color blending, it would be wise to consult a color chart.

Whether or not the frayed head and tail areas of the cloth binding have been recolored, they can be greatly strengthened by the application of a low-gloss polyvinyl acetate adhesive such as Jade No. 454. Apply to the worn area a thin coating of adhesive diluted with water. The index finger makes a sensitive applicator. Dip your finger into the adhesive. If the consistency of the adhesive is correct, only a thin coating of the adhesive will remain on the finger. Rub this adhesive into the interstices of the cloth, and then smooth the frayed threads down into their original position. A second application of the adhesive may be required. The adhesive may look white at first, but when it dries it will be transparent and will have provided a strong seal for the weakened threads. Some brands of polyvinyl acetate emulsion are shiny when dry, which can be disfiguring to the book. Jade No. 454 dries to a dull finish and is less noticeable. Adhesive should be applied only to the top and bottom of the book's spine.

Sealing frayed threads at head of cloth binding

LOOSE LABELS

Loose leather labels should be replaced in position, using undiluted Jade No. 454 adhesive; thin leather responds badly to flour paste because of the paste's considerable moisture content. It is important to line up the label so that the lettering is parallel with the shelf. This is not always easy to do. Labels which are beginning to come loose should be tested. Sometimes they will pop off altogether at the slightest touch. The looseness of a label may be detected sometimes by opening the book in the center and looking down the spine.

Loose paper labels should be reattached. Usually they also need cleaning. Erase gently over the surface. Sometimes one finds a second, clean paper label tipped in at the back of the book, which may be used to replace a soiled torn label.

If the label is detached from the book, adhesive may be applied to the back of the label with a small spatula. The adhesive is applied with a downward pressure, in the same way one butters bread. This keeps the label from moving or tearing. If the label is only partly

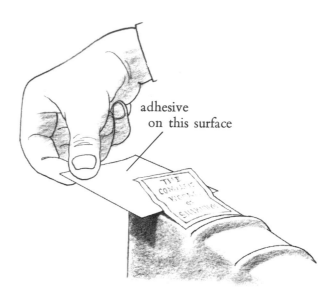

Using slip of paper and adhesive in reattaching labels

loose, apply the adhesive to one side of a piece of well-sized paper, such as typewriting paper. Slide the paper, dry side down, under the loose area of the label. Lay a piece of waxed paper over the label. Press down gently through the waxed paper on the loose area of the label as you pull the paper out from under the label. Then pat down the label through a clean piece of waxed paper to insure good adhesion.

REBUILD CORNERS

The cover of a book is designed to protect the leaves from damage. The corners of the cover take blows that would otherwise be taken by the edges of the leaves themselves. Inevitably, the corners on many books become soft or break open and begin to disintegrate. When the corners are worn away to the level of the leaves, the edges are no longer protected. At this point, a professional binder must take over and either rebind the book or restore the corners.

On the principle of a stitch in time, it is well worthwhile to take the time to preserve the existing corners as long as possible. By the early part of the sixteenth century, pasteboard replaced wood and was in common use as the material for book boards. Early pasteboard was made of sheets of wastepaper, including discarded manuscripts and printer's waste. (Now, of course, book board is made by machine, often using wastepaper which has been repulped.) When earlier pasteboard corners become soft, it is a comparatively easy task to repair them. The materials needed are: Jade No. 403 adhesive, a sharp knife or scalpel, waxed paper, squares of cardboard, and No. 3 Hunt⊕ clips. As demonstrated in the illustration, use the small knife to separate the various layers of paper of which the pasteboard is made. Apply the adhesive between the layers with the knife, then cover the corner with waxed paper, and squeeze the corner between the thumb and index finger to work the adhesive well back between the paper layers. Wipe off any excess adhesive that oozes out of the edges. If the corner holds its shape, let it air-dry. Lay the first book on a board or another book, with its fore edge hanging over the edge of the support below. Lay the second book with its fore edge extending over the spine of the first, etc. If the layers of paper insist on opening up again before the adhesive has dried, the following procedure may be used: Cover the corner with waxed paper, place pieces of cardboard on both sides of the corner, and slide a clip over the cardboard to hold the corner in shape until it has dried for some time. The special precautions which should be taken when rebuilding the corners of old leather books will be discussed later in this pamphlet. Occasionally, one finds a corner whose covering is intact but which is very soft under the covering. Here a decision must be made. It may be worthwhile to cut open the covering material, rebuild the board underneath, and then fit the covering back into position again. Often one will find a binding with broken corners whose board has become powdery. The fibers of the board have doubtless deteriorated; when such a corner breaks away, it must be repaired by a professional binder. Put the book aside in the WRITE-UP pile. When the corner of the wooden board of an early binding breaks, it must be rebuilt by a professional binder.

VELLUM AND ALUM-TAWED LEATHER BINDINGS

Vellum bindings present many special problems. Because of the hygroscopic nature of this material, these bindings respond to changes in humidity to such a degree that the covers will often become badly warped in the winter and then flatten out in the summer. Air-conditioning throughout the year is highly desirable for

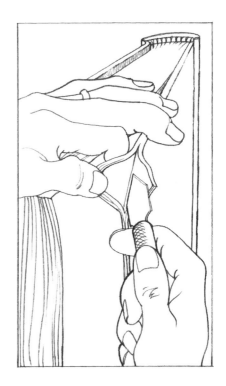

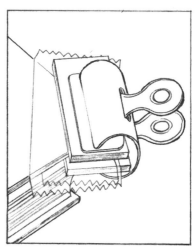

Rebuilding broken corners

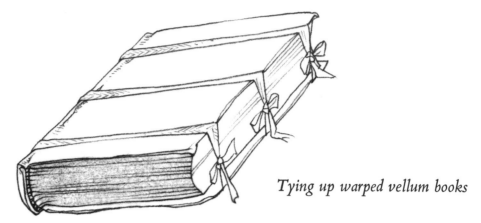

Tying up warped vellum books

vellum books. Otherwise, they should be kept under constant pressure in slipcases, which keep the sides from reacting so rapidly to changes in humidity. Such bindings may have been warped many times in the past, even though they are now flat and stored in an air-conditioned environment. Particular attention should be given to cleaning these books, since dust may have sifted in between the pages. Check through the pages and look at the outside. Dust may have accumulated on the outer cover or even penetrated the pores of the vellum.

In general, washing vellum is not recommended. If there is a handwritten title, washing is likely to reduce its clarity. Gold stamping or tooling on vellum is particularly susceptible to being removed by washing. Saddle soap⊕ removes dirt from vellum effectively, but since a moist cloth must be used in the process of application, there is still danger of dimming the title. Cleaning the vellum with the Pink Pearl or the Magic-Rub eraser is effective and allows the surface to retain its patina of age.

Sometimes entire shelves of vellum books will be found to have warped. This condition can create a shelving problem, since the covers will not close and the books cannot be lined up. To deal with this problem, the following procedure is recommended. Wait until there has been a period of humid weather. One may then find that the vellum covers have absorbed enough moisture from the air to permit the warping covers to return to their normal condition. If this is the case, the books can be tied up firmly to help maintain the covers in their unwarped condition. Use a woven tape⊕ for tying, rather than a round cord which might cut into the boards. Tie the tape with a bowknot that is easy to open.

Vellum and tawed leather absorb very little oil, and we do not recommend oiling these materials.

Alum-tawed bindings should not be washed. The materials used in their manufacture are water-soluble and are easily removed, rendering the skin subject to decay. Clean these bindings with an eraser.

STAPLES

The staples in pamphlets rust during humid weather in a non-air-conditioned library. The rust eventually destroys the paper underneath. Therefore, we suggest that the staples be removed and that the pamphlets be resewn with thread. So far we have found no

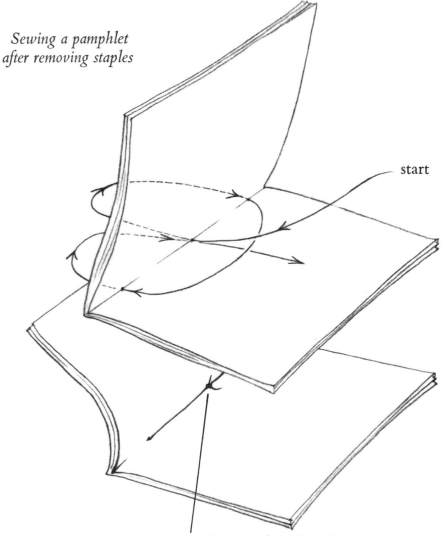

Sewing a pamphlet after removing staples

start

square knot tied over other thread

staple-remover that is safe for use on delicate materials. Slip the end of an ordinary table knife under each prong of the staple, lift the prongs up, and pull the staple out from the other side.

To resew a pamphlet, thread a needle with unbleached linen thread⊕ and push the needle through the center of the inside fold to the outside, leaving a four-inch tail. Push the needle into the fold from the outside about one inch below the head of the pamphlet; then push the needle out from the inside of the fold about one inch from the tail of the pamphlet. Now insert the needle again in the first hole in the center of the pamphlet. Have the two ends of the thread on opposite sides of the long center stitch. Tie a square knot, test it, then cut the thread off leaving a one-fourth-inch tail.

WRITE-UP

In any collection some books are likely to be found that require treatment by a professional binder or restorer. If, for instance, the boards are detached, the joints cracking, the leaves falling out, or the spine detached or missing, the book will obviously need to be rebound, or restored, or protected by a container. An untrained worker should not attempt such repairs. Books that require special treatment should be put aside under the WRITE-UP label. Before being reshelved, the books may be discussed with the librarian or collector, who might wish to make immediate decisions about the treatment; otherwise, a record should be made indicating the nature of the problem before the book is reshelved.

In keeping records of books that need further work, we have found the following procedure convenient: Using 3 × 5-inch slips of bond paper and carbon paper cut to the same size, make an original and one copy of the record for each title. The entry should indicate the author, short title, number of volumes in the set, call number or shelf position, and a short description of the condition. Separate the slips and file. One set can be arranged under the author or call number, and the other according to the type of work needed.

TIE-UP

After problem books have been written up for further repair, certain books will be found that are too weak to be replaced on the shelf without some support. If the joints of a book have broken or if the boards have become detached, the book may still be replaced on the shelf if it is properly tied up. We suggest tying the book with flat cotton tape. Wrap the tape around the book from the top to the bottom and then from the spine to the fore edge as one would tie a package. Tie a bowknot at the fore edge so that the knot will not be visible when the book is shelved and will not be in a position to catch on adjacent books.

Tying up a book that has loose boards

WRAP-UP

Some books need even more protection. If leaves are loose, or if boards are missing, it is safer to wrap the book in acid-free paper, tie it up four ways with flat cotton tape, and write the author, title, and call number on the outside. The package can be either reshelved or stored away until further action can be taken. The wrapping is important to prevent further damage to leaves or loss of vital parts of the binding.

TREATMENT OF LEATHER WITH POTASSIUM LACTATE SOLUTION

The potassium lactate treatment was earlier referred to as the first treatment that should be given to leather bindings. (It should be understood that in this section and the following sections through the end of the text on page 54, "leather" excludes alum-tawed leather. The reader will remember that alum-tawed leather bindings were separated from the other leather bindings earlier, together with the cloth, paper, and vellum bindings.) We will attempt a brief explanation of this treatment and why it should be applied to all leather bindings that are still in a condition to be saved. There is a considerable body of literature on this subject, some of which we refer to in the Bibliography, for those who would like to understand the process more thoroughly. H. J. Plenderleith says in *The Preservation of Leather Bookbindings* [33]:

The main cause of the decay of leather is the absence of an ingredient (natural or artificial) which protects the tissue from the action of sulphuric acid which is formed in all leather (in time) by absorption and oxidation of sulphur dioxide, and when this preventive ingredient is present vegetable tanned leathers can resist oxidation in the presence of sulphuric acid and do not deteriorate. No leather can be relied upon to be durable unless it is so protected.

Also J. S. Rogers and C. W. Beebe in *Leather Bookbindings: How To Preserve Them* [34] have this to say:

The chief cause of decay of leather bookbindings is high acidity in the leather. A secondary cause is lack of oil or grease in the leather. High acidity in leather is sometimes attributed to the addition of excessive acid during the manufacturing process.

More often, the high acidity is caused by absorption of acidic gases from polluted atmospheres. These acid contaminants are sulphur compounds produced by the burning of coal, gas or other sulphur-containing materials. When the acidic gases are absorbed, they produce sulphuric acid, which decomposes leather . . . [One] of the methods that can be used to make leather acid resistant . . . [is the] inclusion of a buffering agent. The buffering agent is usually the sodium or potassium salt of tartaric or lactic acid.

Plenderleith points out that the natural protective salts present in properly tanned leather are water-soluble. If the binder sponged the leather with water in the process of covering the book, or if the binding has ever been washed in an attempt to clean it, the protective salts may have been washed out. It is also possible that the salts may have been removed from the leather in the tanning process.

The British Museum Laboratory recommends that a protective salt solution be applied to all leather that is still in good enough condition to be saved, as the first step in a regular program of preservative treatment. The formula for this solution in the 1947 edition of the booklet *The Preservation of Leather Bookbindings* [33] by H. J. Plenderleith is the one I prefer. It consists of 7 per cent potassium lactate in distilled water with 0.25 per cent paranitrophenol⊕ added to protect the solution and the leather from mold. *

The effectiveness of this treatment has been established beyond any doubt by impartial tests, including the accelerated aging tests described and pictured in Plenderleith's booklet. Library conservators have been using the potassium lactate formula on leather books for over twenty years, and during this time no known harmful side effects, or spew on the surface, have been observed.

* As an alternative to the 0.25 per cent paranitrophenol, A. D. Baynes-Cope, Principal Scientific Officer, British Museum Research Laboratory, has suggested the use of a 0.007 per cent solution of orthophenylphenol as a mold inhibitor in the potassium lactate solution.

We do offer several warnings: Do not use the solution on suede bindings or on leather that has become powdery. If you suspect that the leather is too powdery to be treated, we suggest that you apply a small amount of the solution to an inconspicuous spot which looks red and dusty. If, after it has dried, the leather has been blackened, do not use the formula on the rest of the binding. The blackening occurs as a result of the action of the water in the formula on the powdery leather, rather than from the potassium lactate or paranitrophenol. Water alone would have an identical effect on such deteriorated leather.

Collectors and curators often assume that leather bindings that are in apparently good condition are not yet ready for treatment. On the contrary, those which are in apparently good condition are the very ones that will benefit most from early preventive treatment.

In preparing to treat leather bindings with the potassium lactate solution, assemble the following: a flat, heavy dish such as a heavy, glass ash tray, a bottle of potassium lactate solution, a terry-cloth towel, and some small pieces of terry cloth about six inches square, or pads of absorbent cotton.

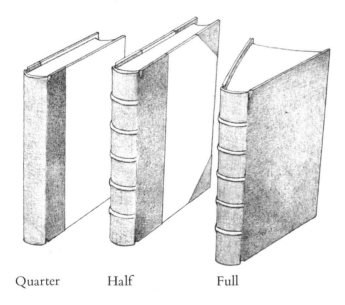

Quarter   Half   Full

Quarter-, half-, and full-leather bindings

Examine the leather books and remove the suede and powdery leather bindings for later treatment. Then separate the full-leather bindings from the half- and quarter-leather bindings. It is safer to treat these categories separately because the half- and quarter-leather bindings will need special care in order to prevent staining of the cloth or paper sides. It is better to treat them first while the work surfaces are clean.

Pour some of the potassium lactate solution into the flat dish. Fold in the raw edges of the terry cloth to make a compact pad. Dip the pad in the potassium lactate solution. Squeeze out the excess just enough to prevent the pad from dripping. Pick up a quarter- or a half-leather binding with your left hand. Concentrate on keeping the

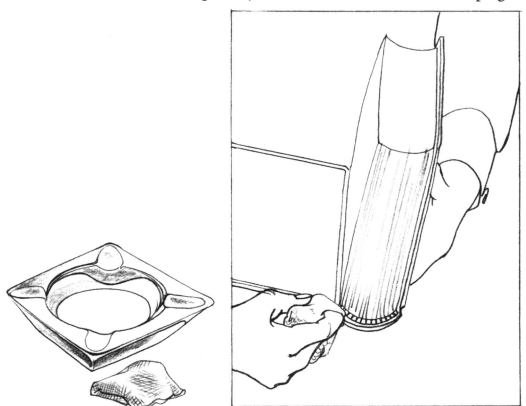

Treating a leather binding with potassium lactate solution

left hand clean and dry. Finger rings should be removed from both hands to prevent damage to the leather when it is wet. When holding the book, many workers find it convenient to open the covers slightly and to grasp the body of the pages while treating the outer cover.

Apply the pad wet with the potassium lactate solution to the leather areas. Use a patting rather than a rubbing motion, since rubbing may dull or loosen the gold. Apply the solution to the leather only—not to the cloth or paper sides. The covers may be opened somewhat in order to treat the leather that is turned in on the inside of the covers (the turn-ins). Now concentrate on applying the solution to the head and tail caps and especially to the turn-in of the leather at the top and bottom of the hinge area. This area is where the first signs of deterioration will be seen, and it is important that this be given all the protection possible. Examine the leather after you have gone over it with the solution. If the liquid has been absorbed by the leather, you may set the book down on its tail with the boards slightly open and let it air-dry. All precautions should be taken to prevent the books from falling off the table. Proceed with the rest of the books. If you observe that the solution has not been absorbed by the leather but is standing up in beads on the surface, wipe over the surface of the leather with a terry-cloth towel. The solution has not penetrated because the leather probably has been coated with varnish or wax. If the potassium lactate is allowed to dry in beads, the surface of the leather may become spotted. These spots are difficult to remove.

Plenderleith suggests that the treated leather be allowed to dry for twenty-four hours. Of course, this drying time will depend on ambient conditions of temperature and relative humidity. In a hot, dry atmosphere one can expect the treated leather to dry more quickly.

EXTERIOR TREATMENT OF QUARTER-, HALF-, OR FULL-LEATHER BINDINGS

When the potassium lactate application is dry, examine the books for exterior treatment. You should postpone inside treatment until the leather has been oiled and the hinges are more flexible. Repair soft and broken corners with flour paste.

Reattach loose tabs of leather and loose labels with an adhesive whose water content is low, such as Jade No. 454. Recolor rubbed edges and chipped areas at head, tail, and corner, using a safe coloring agent such as Dr. Martin's Synchromatic Transparent Water Colors. Avoid coloring over the stamping or tooling. Soft or broken corners should be repaired as described earlier. When rebuilding broken corners, remember that old leather has a tendency to turn black when water-soaked. Avoid using waxed paper and Hunt clips to hold layers of the board together while they dry, unless absolutely necessary. If it is necessary to clamp the corners, remove the clip and the waxed paper after a few minutes to be sure the leather is not turning dark. Erase soiled cloth sides with Pink Pearl or other erasers. Considerable dirt can be removed from the leather with potassium lactate solution; if it is extremely dirty, however, it may be cleaned with saddle soap. Care should be taken not to use too much water in applying the soap, particularly if the leather surface is porous or has become powdery. It should not, of course, be used on suede bindings. Also, avoid concentrated rubbing over gold-tooled areas. The leather should then be carefully wiped with a soft cloth and thoroughly dried. If the leather has a pronounced grain, the saddle soap will have a tendency to settle into the pores, dry, and present a whitish appearance. In order to prevent this, the dried surface should be gone over with a soft brush to remove any residual soap. After the cleaning (if any) is done and these repairs are made, the leather is ready to be treated with a leather dressing.

SELECTING A LEATHER DRESSING

Some authorities recommend treating leather with the British Museum Leather Dressing, after it has been protected with the potassium lactate solution. This formula contains a mixture of anhydrous lanolin, cedarwood oil, beeswax, and hexane. There are several serious disadvantages to this formula. First, it is a fire hazard, since the solvent, hexane, is flammable. Second, it can be a health hazard if not used in a work area that is properly ventilated, since prolonged exposure to its fumes may cause headaches and nausea. As far as the leather itself is concerned, the formula has also caused many problems. The proportion of beeswax in the original formula is likely to cause the leather to be quite sticky, even after strenuous polishing. Some libraries report books sticking together on the shelves after treatment with this formula. We have also heard reports that regular use of the formula has caused wax to build up and harden on the surface, and then chip off, taking some of the surface leather with it.

Rogers and Beebe present eight formulas for leather dressings in their booklet *Leather Bookbindings: How To Preserve Them* [34]. Of these eight, the first two contain lanolin, water, Japan wax, and sodium stearate. We do not recommend these two formulas. There is sufficient water in the mixtures to cause excessive blackening if applied to powdery leather. More serious trouble shows up with both of these formulas after a week or so. If they have been applied to dark-colored, deep-grained goatskin leather, a white deposit is likely to appear in the grain. This fill-in is almost impossible to remove. It does not respond to scrubbing with solvents, detergents, or water. Only very vigorous brushing with a stiff toothbrush dipped in potassium lactate solution will remove some of the swirls or reduce discoloration.

Formula three contains neat's-foot oil, lanolin, Japan wax, and sodium stearate; and formula four contains lanolin, sperm oil, Japan wax, and sodium stearate. These lack the water contained in the first two formulas, but they both contain Japan wax and sodium stearate which appear to produce disfiguring fill-in in the pores of the leather. Formula seven is pure petrolatum. There are those who believe that a mineral oil should not be used on an animal skin. Formula eight is saddle soap, which is excellent for cleaning smooth leather and which has a beneficial effect on leather as far as its pH value is concerned, but which does not lubricate the leather to any noticeable degree. Formula five is a mixture of neat's-foot oil and castor oil, and formula six a mixture of neat's-foot oil and anhydrous lanolin. Each one of the above formulas has its supporters.

At the present time, we recommend the use of formula six⊕ as described in the Rogers and Beebe booklet [34]: a mixture of 60 per cent neat's-foot oil, 20° C. cold test, and 40 per cent anhydrous lanolin. On the basis of laboratory tests and personal observation, this preparation is readily absorbed by leather, has no embrittling effect, is applied to leather very easily, and presents neither a fire hazard nor a health hazard to the worker. The oil can be purchased already mixed, or the materials can be bought at a chemical supply house and mixed in the following manner: Warm the lanolin in a double boiler until it is melted. Add the neat's-foot oil and stir until the mixture is uniformly blended. It will form a soft salve.

The two-step treatment we have suggested for the preservation of leather—potassium lactate solution first, followed by a mixture of neat's-foot oil and anhydrous lanolin (with any necessary cleaning between the two)—is the one we favor at the present time. We hope the two applications may be reduced to one at some future time by a combination of ingredients that will simultaneously retard decay and lubricate, with a mold inhibitor and insecticide included for additional protection. We also hope that the need for frequency of treatment will be reduced.

APPLYING THE LEATHER DRESSING

The oil can be poured into a heavy, flat dish, such as the glass ash tray used for the potassium lactate solution. The oil can be applied with a cloth pad, as described previously for the application of potassium lactate, or a flat paint brush. The pad permits careful application of the oil. This is particularly important in treating half- and quarter-bindings, where care must be taken to keep oil off paper or cloth sides. An accidental spot should be removed at once with a wad of cotton dampened with toluene or hexane. Start oiling the half- and quarter-leather bindings first. It is important to keep one hand clean and free of oil while handling the books so as to avoid marking the paper or cloth sides with oily fingerprints. Some workers hold the book by the paper sides. Others prefer to open the covers enough to hold the book by the inside pages (the body of the book). Because of the risk of getting oil on the pages of the books, we do not attempt to oil the leather turn-ins on the inside of the boards. However, we do oil the leather on the edges of the boards and the leather headcaps. A piece of unprinted newsprint or a manila second sheet between the end papers will help keep the pages free of oil. Full-leather bindings may be oiled with the hand as an applicator. Apply the mixture generously. Almost all leather, except that which has been varnished or coated with wax, will absorb a great deal of oil if left to stand for two days or more. After the oil has been applied, lay the book on its side, on a piece of manila paper. Put book number two on top of number one, but place protective sheets of the manila paper or blank newsprint between them. With the half-leather bindings it is obvious that two such sheets are needed to prevent oil from seeping through from one book to another and spotting the cloth or paper sides of the books. Protective sheets are also used between full-leather bindings to prevent them from sticking together while the oil is still on the surface. Continue piling the oiled books on top of one another with two manila sheets between each book. The piles must not be so high that there is danger of books toppling. Be sure larger books are near the bottom, and start a new pile before there is any sign of unsteadiness. Twelve to fifteen inches is about the maximum safe height for average-sized books. Later these piles can be moved to an empty shelf or placed on the floor under worktables. They should remain undisturbed for at least two days to permit the oil to penetrate as fully as possible.

A special note about oil: Oil will darken porous leather. If the leather has a very evenly polished surface, or if it has been varnished or waxed, the oil will not darken it appreciably. However, on such a

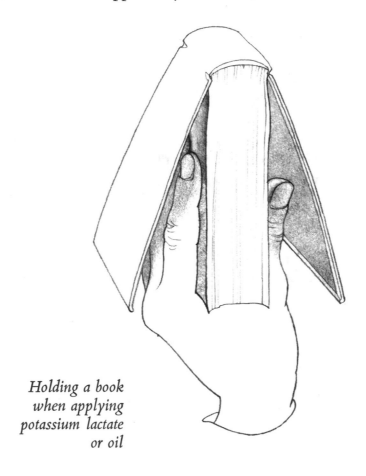

*Holding a book
when applying
potassium lactate
or oil*

surface, wherever there is a scratch, natural blemish, or porous area, the oil will penetrate more fully and consequently cause the leather to darken unevenly. On old bindings such uneven darkening blends in with the tree-calf patterning, or the sprinkling on the sides, and adds to the charm of the books. However, in some instances, such as modern art bindings, uneven darkening will be disfiguring.

When preparing to treat such modern bindings, the following procedure is recommended: Immediately after the leather has been treated with the potassium lactate solution, examine the surface in a good light. If the liquid has penetrated the leather unevenly, try saturating the surface with more of the potassium lactate solution. If the solution still will not penetrate the leather surface evenly, then you can be sure that the oil will not penetrate the surface evenly. While the darkening caused by the potassium lactate solution will disappear, the discoloration caused by the uneven penetration of the oil will remain. Therefore, put such books aside under a MINIMUM OIL label.

When preparing to oil books labeled MINIMUM OIL, be sure you are working in a good light. Dip a wad of cotton in the neat's-foot oil and lanolin mixture. Squeeze out as much excess oil as possible. Make sure there are no stray drops of oil on your hands; then go over the surface of the leather rapidly, using a circular motion. This first oiling with the slightly oily cotton wad appears to act as a sizing. After all the MINIMUM OIL books have been treated in this manner, you may go back and very cautiously re-oil the leather with slightly more oil.

POLISHING

After two or more days, the books are ready to be polished. We find that soft terry-cloth towels are rough enough to buff up the books nicely and yet not so rough that they damage the surface of the leather. Some workers feel that cheesecloth is safer for polishing delicate old leather. Polish all the oiled surfaces and be sure to remove any residue of oil or lint from either side of the bands. Change the towels often enough so that there is no danger of the towel depositing oil marks on the paper or cloth sides of half-leather books. After polishing, the books should go into the INSPECT pile.

INSPECTING OILED BOOKS

Some books may appear dull and have areas that look dry. These should receive another coat of oil and stand for several days. Inspect for tags of leather that may have come loose. These should be re-attached. Occasionally, chips of leather will have fallen off. Such chipped areas can be made less conspicuous by being touched up with water color, which seems to conceal blemishes even after oiling. Although the area is likely to look a little dull when the color is dry, this can be corrected by rubbing oil over the colored area and wiping it off with a cloth. Check again for any accidental oil stains and remove them with toluene or hexane on a wad of cotton.

SUEDE AND VERY POWDERY LEATHER BINDINGS

Suede was sometimes used as a binding material for ledgers and blank books during the later part of the eighteenth and early part of the nineteenth centuries. The suede used for these bindings was usually a reverse calf, rather than a split sheepskin. This leather is usually rather powdery. The water in the potassium lactate solution is likely to darken and spot the suede. We have had some success in consolidating the surface of such leather by spraying it with Krylon. A number of light coats can be applied without radically changing the appearance of the suede. The material can then be handled without disintegrating into powder. Modern suede which is made of split sheepskin is likely to have disintegrated beyond restorability. Leather bindings that have become so powdery that it is obvious the covering material cannot be restored by oiling alone can also be sprayed with Krylon.

INTERIOR TREATMENT OF LEATHER BINDINGS

After the leather bindings have been given a complete exterior treatment and the hinges have had a chance to become more flexible, inspect and repair the inside of the books. Follow the same procedure used in the inspection and repair of cloth, paper, tawed leather, and vellum bindings. A separate set of heavy labels and a separate work area are advisable for leather treatment. No matter how good the condition of the leather may be, color does rub off and powdery areas leave a residue on the table which can disfigure more sensitive cloth and paper bindings. The leather volumes may be bookplated and checked for enclosures and acid transfer. Where leather turn-ins are staining the flyleaves, a barrier sheet may be inserted between the end papers. Slit unopened leaves if this is appropriate. Leather bindings seldom need tightening, except for occasional leather case bindings. Leather bindings whose condition is too deteriorated for treatment during the refurbishing program should be put aside under the WRITE-UP label. They can then be either tied up or wrapped. The leather books may now be shelved.

HOW OFTEN SHOULD BOOKS BE TREATED?

Books should be cleaned whenever they become dusty. Leather bindings (with those exceptions noted throughout the text) should be treated with potassium lactate solution and oiled whenever they appear dry. The amount of dust they accumulate and the rapidity with which they appear to dry out will depend on the geographical location and construction of the library. Books kept in an air-conditioned library which also has a complete air-purification system will need treatment very seldom. Books stored in the country far from sources of air pollution will also stay clean and chemically stable for a long time. Books housed in a non-air-conditioned library in an industrial area will need frequent cleaning and treatment.

No amount of treatment will restore a leather binding that has begun to deteriorate. Oil will serve to slow down powdering of the leather but not chemical deterioration. Treatment should be given to leather while it is still in good condition. The better the condition of the leather, the more worthwhile the treatment is.

We recommend that all books be inspected at least every two years for potential treatment. The treatment should in any case not be postponed for more than five years.

Appendix 1
Work Flow Diagram

Normal routine to follow in refurbishing a collection

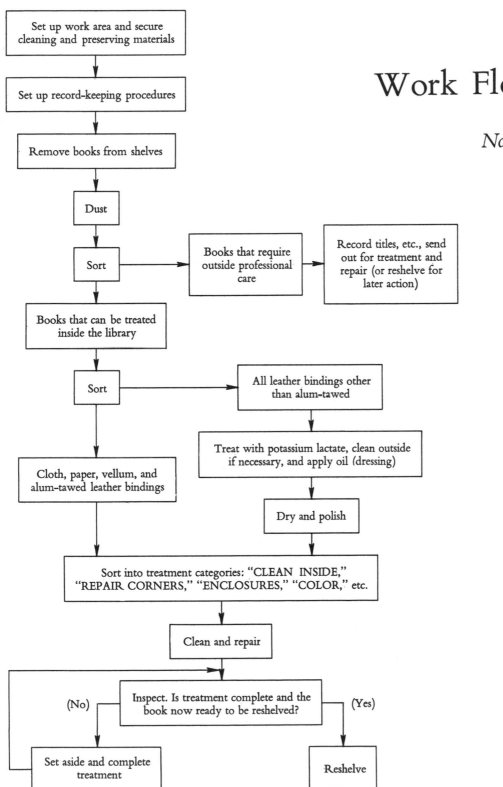

Set up work area and secure cleaning and preserving materials

Set up record-keeping procedures

Remove books from shelves

Dust

Sort → Books that require outside professional care → Record titles, etc., send out for treatment and repair (or reshelve for later action)

Books that can be treated inside the library

Sort → All leather bindings other than alum-tawed → Treat with potassium lactate, clean outside if necessary, and apply oil (dressing) → Dry and polish

Cloth, paper, vellum, and alum-tawed leather bindings

Sort into treatment categories: "CLEAN INSIDE," "REPAIR CORNERS," "ENCLOSURES," "COLOR," etc.

Clean and repair

Inspect. Is treatment complete and the book now ready to be reshelved?

(No) Set aside and complete treatment

(Yes) Reshelve

Appendix 2
Supplies and Equipment

The supplies and equipment listed below are those which are specified in the text by the symbol ⊕. As such, they are those used by the author, Mrs. Horton, or known by her to be in general use and to perform in an acceptable manner.

The listing of such supplies and equipment does not, however, imply endorsement or recommendation of these products by the American Library Association or the Library Technology Program. The scope of the first phase of the project "Conservation of Library Materials" did not permit comprehensive testing and analysis of all supplies and equipment actually used or potentially usable in cleaning and preserving bindings and related materials. However, some of the materials listed below were tested insofar as their safety for use on various bookmaking materials is concerned. A summary of the test methods and results follows on pages 62–64.

The list of supplies and equipment is followed on page 60 by a detailed listing of those sources of supply referenced under the product.

ADHESIVES

Polyvinyl Acetate Emulsion Adhesive No. 403 (Jade No. 403)
    Manufactured by Jade Adhesives, Inc., 2929 North Campbell Avenue, Chicago, Illinois 60618.
    Sold by TLS.

Polyvinyl Acetate Emulsion Adhesive No. 454 (Jade No. 454)
    Manufactured by Jade Adhesives, Inc., 2929 North Campbell Avenue, Chicago, Illinois 60618.
    Sold by TLS.

Wheat Paste No. 6
    Manufactured by Samuel Schweitzer Co., 660 West Lake Street, Chicago, Illinois 60606.
    Sold by TLS.

CLEANING SUPPLIES

Absorene Wall Paper Cleaner
   Manufactured by Absorene Manufacturing Company, Inc., 1609 North
      14th Street, St. Louis, Missouri 63106.
   Sold by wallpaper stores.

Delkote Bookleen, liquid and gel
   Manufactured by Delkote, Inc., 76 South Virginia Avenue, Penns
      Grove, New Jersey 08069.
   Sold by Delkote, Inc., NBC, and TLS.

Demco Book Cleaner
   Manufactured and sold by Demco Educational Corporation, 2120
      Fordem Avenue, Madison, Wisconsin 53701.

Endust
   Manufactured by The Drackett Company, 5020 Spring Grove Avenue,
      Cincinnati, Ohio 45232.
   Sold by grocery and hardware stores.

Goddard's Book Restorer for Cloth Bindings
   Manufactured by J. Goddard & Sons, Ltd., Leicester, England (U.S.
      sales office: 299 Madison Avenue, New York, New York 10017).
   Sold by department and hardware stores.

Magic-Rub Erasers
   Manufactured by A. W. Faber-Castell Pencil Company, Inc., Dickerson
      and Bittman Streets, Newark, New Jersey 07103.
   Sold by art and stationery stores and TLS.

One-Wipe Dust Cloths (Bon Ami)
   Manufactured by Standard Household Products Corporation, 51 Gar-
      field, Holyoke, Massachusetts 01040.
   Sold by grocery and hardware stores and TLS.

Opaline Cleaner
   Manufactured by Durasol Drug & Chemical Company, 325 Marginal
      Street, East Boston, Massachusetts 02128.
   Sold by art supply stores and TLS.

Pink Pearl Erasers No. 101
   Manufactured by Eberhard Faber Inc., Crestwood, Wilkes-Barre,
      Pennsylvania 18703.
   Sold by art supply or stationery stores and TLS.

EQUIPMENT

Combination Press
Can be made at home following directions in Klinefelter's *Bookbinding Made Easy* [21].
Manufactured and sold by TLS.

Glue-Fast BX Label Gluer
Sold by TLS.

Potdevin Label Paster
Manufactured and sold by Potdevin Machine Company, 233 North Street, Teterboro, New Jersey 07608.

LEATHER PRESERVATIVES AND CLEANERS

Formula No. 6 Leather Dressing
(40 per cent anhydrous lanolin and 60 per cent neat's-foot oil)
May be mixed from ingredients bought from chemical supply houses such as ADC and FSC.
Mixed and sold by ADC, NL, and TLS.

Leather Protector (Potassium Lactate Solution)
(7 per cent potassium lactate and 0.25 per cent paranitrophenol)
May be mixed from ingredients bought from chemical supply houses such as ADC and FSC.
Mixed and sold by ADC, NL, and TLS.

Propert's Leather and Saddle Soap
Manufactured by Propert, Ltd., Burlington Lane, London W4, England.
Sold by shoe-repair shops, saddle shops.

PAPER FOR MENDING AND HINGES

Dennison's Transparent Mending Tape
Manufactured by Dennison Manufacturing Company, 67 Ford Avenue, Framingham, Massachusetts 01701.
Sold by party-favor shops and library-supply companies, and TLS.

Green's 105 Lens Tissue
Manufactured by J. Barcham Green Ltd., Hayle Mill, Maidstone, Kent, England.
Sold by ANW, AAM, and TLS.

Sekishu and Shizuoka Paper
Sold by ANW and TLS.

TOOLS AND MISCELLANEOUS SUPPLIES

Bone Folders
   Sold by TLS.

Brayers
   Sold by art supply stores and TLS.

Brushes
   Sold by GBL, NBC, and TLS.

Dr. Martin's Synchromatic Transparent Water Colors
   Manufactured by B. Aronstein & Company, 41-02A 162d Street, Flush-
      ing, New York 11358.
   Sold by art supply stores and TLS.

Hunt Clips No. 3
   Manufactured by Hunt Manufacturing Company, 1405 Locust Street,
      Philadelphia, Pennsylvania 19102.
   Sold by art supply stores and TLS.

Krylon No. 1301
   Manufactured by Borden Chemical Company, Consumer Products
      Division, 350 Madison Avenue, New York, New York 10017.

Linen Thread, unbleached
   Sold by GBL, NBC, ES, and TLS.

Mylar Sheeting
   Sold by TLS.

Woven Cotton Tape
   Sold by TLS.

Appendix 3
Sources of Supply

The sources-of-supply listing has been prepared by the author. There may be other sources that can supply the material referred to in this pamphlet. Any firm not included in this listing which sells such materials is invited to advise the Library Technology Program of this fact so that the listing may be supplemented. Requests for inclusion in the listing should indicate the specific material, or materials, handled.

Code

AAM   Aiko's Art Materials Import
        714 North Wabash Avenue
        Chicago, Illinois 60611

ADC   Amend Drug & Chemical Co., Inc.
        117 East 24th Street
        New York, New York 10010

ANW   Andrews-Nelson-Whitehead
        7 Laight Street
        New York, New York 10013

ES   Ernest Schaefer, Inc.
        731 Lehigh Avenue
        Union, New Jersey 07083

FSC   Fisher Scientific Company
        711 Forbes Avenue
        Pittsburgh, Pennsylvania 15219

        Branches elsewhere in the United States.

GBL   Gane Brothers and Lane Inc.
        1335 West Lake Street
        Chicago, Illinois 60607

        Branches elsewhere in the United States.

NBC   Nevins Bookcrafts
       2622 West 7th Street
       Los Angeles, California 90057

NL   The Newberry Library
       60 West Walton Street
       Chicago, Illinois 60610

TLS   Technical Library Service
       104 Fifth Avenue
       New York, New York 10011

Appendix 4
Summary of Test Report

A number of commercially available products, including wall-paper cleaners, erasers, cleaning cloths, book-cleaning solutions, leather dressings, and the like, were known by the author of this book to be effective in the cleaning and conditioning of book-making materials. As far as could be determined, however, no objective, independent tests had been made of these products to determine whether their use involved the leaving of any harmful residues on the treated materials which might result in their damage or deterioration.

At the request of the Library Technology Program, therefore, a total of seventeen products was subjected to various tests to determine their effect, over varying periods of time, on a carefully selected range of bookmaking materials. A summary of the test procedures and results follows. Anyone desiring a detailed account of the actual test results for each product may request them from the Library Technology Program, American Library Association, Chicago.

The bookmaking materials to which the various products to be tested were applied consisted of both wood- and rag-pulp paper, vellum, and leather. The Library Technology Program supplied both the bookmaking materials and the products to be tested.

In the tests made on paper, the tested products were used according to the manufacturers' directions on two strips of wood-pulp paper and two strips of rag-pulp paper. Two untreated strips of wood-pulp paper and two of rag-pulp paper were retained as controls. One of each of the treated strips and one each of the untreated (control) strips were then artificially aged to the equivalent of 225 years by a heat-treatment accelerated aging test devised and used by the National Bureau of Standards (this test is now incorporated in TAPPI [Technical Association of Pulp and Paper Industries] test method T 453 ts-63). Available for test purposes, therefore, were four strips of paper for each product tested: an unaged, treated wood-pulp paper; an aged, treated wood-pulp paper; an unaged, treated rag-pulp paper; and an aged, treated rag-pulp paper. All treated paper strips and all untreated control strips were subjected to the same four tests in order to determine what effect, if any, the products being tested had on them:

1. The M.I.T. Folding-Endurance Test
2. A tear-resistance test
3. A pH test (of acidity or alkalinity)
4. A microscopical examination

The samples were conditioned under standard conditions of temperature and humidity as specified in TAPPI test method T 402 os-49, and were cut to a uniform size with the long side in the machine direction (as determined by TAPPI test method T 409 m-35).

The M.I.T. Folding-Endurance Test (TAPPI test method T 423 m-50) is a standard one in the industry: tension is placed on a sample by the addition of a weight, and the number of double folds that can be made before the sample breaks is counted. (The load used by us for the rag-pulp paper was 1 kg; for the wood-pulp paper, 0.4 kg.) Several tests are run on each sample.

The tear-resistance apparatus used was similar to the Elmendorf Tear-Resistance Test apparatus as specified in TAPPI test method T 414 ts-65. (Because the small sample size did not permit the use of the Elmendorf machine, a special machine was constructed for the tests, using the same principle as the Elmendorf.) In the testing of tear-resistance, the weight necessary to continue an initial tear is measured. The greater the weight required, of course, the greater the tear-resistance of the paper.

The pH (acidity/alkalinity) of the samples was determined according to the TAPPI Cold Extraction Procedure (as specified in TAPPI Routine Control Method RC-29 pH of Paper [Cold Extract]).

Microscopical examination involved actual viewing of the fibers in the samples for evidence of chemical or physical damage.

The vellum and leather samples were tested for changes in pH by a modification of ACLA (American Leather Chemists' Association)

Official Method B20. High acidity in these materials leads to their early deterioration. Changes in color before and after treatment were also noted, but any color changes were considered secondary to the pH content. These materials were also examined microscopically.

Only those tested products which were judged by us to be safe when used with reasonable care according to the manufacturers' directions have been recommended for use by the author in this volume. In some cases these products actually improved the sample materials, usually by increasing their alkalinity, which helps to counter the undesirable effects of acidic airborne substances.

WALTER C. MCCRONE ASSOCIATES, INC.

Glossary

Acid Migration

The transfer of acid from an acid material, such as ground-wood paper, to a less-acid material when the two are stored in contact with each other. The transfer will usually cause the less-acid material to become stained and weakened; called also *acid transfer*.

Alum-tawed Leather

Leather (usually pigskin) treated with alum instead of tanbark or other tanning agents. The surface resembles vellum in its hardness, except for the typical pigskin pores. These skins are often found on books bound from the twelfth century through the Renaissance and have demonstrated great durability and permanence. *See also* Leather.

Archival Lamination—See Cellulose Acetate Film Lamination

Backbone

The edge of a book along which the sections are secured together in binding; the part that shows as the book ordinarily stands on a shelf and that is often lettered with the title and the author's and publisher's names; called also *back, backstrip, shelfback, spine*.

Barrier Sheets

Pieces of well-sized paper used as barriers to prevent migration of acid or oil from one material to another.

Binder's Board

A general term for the pulped materials pressed into stiff, flat, smooth sheets of various thicknesses; used for the cover of a book, under the cloth, leather, or any other material. Also called *book board*.

Board Paper—See End Paper

Bolt

The uncut fold of paper at the head, fore edge, and foot of a signature.

Book Board—See Binder's Board

Book Jacket

A detachable, protective wrapper for a book typically consisting of a rectangular sheet of paper elaborately printed with descriptive or promotional material, cut flush at head and foot, and folded around the binding with ends tucked between cover board and free end paper; called also *book wrapper, dust cover, dust jacket, dust wrapper.*

Bookplate

A book owner's identification label which is usually printed, has a distinctive design, and is usually pasted to the inside front cover of a book; called also *ex libris.*

Bosses

Brass or other metal knobs fastened upon the boards of books for ornament or protection of the covering materials.

Brass-bound Boards

Wooden pressing boards edged with a brass strip which projects about one-sixteenth inch beyond the face of the board, used by binders for defining the groove in a case binding; called also *brass-edged boards.*

Brayer

A printer's hand inking roller.

Bristol Board

A thin paperboard with a smooth surface suitable for writing or printing, generally of .006-inch thickness or more. Index cards are a familiar example.

C Clamp

A C-shaped general-purpose clamp that clamps between the open ends of the C by means of a long flat-ended screw that threads through one end and presses the clamped material against the other end.

Call Number

A combination of characters assigned to a library book to indicate its place on the shelf relative to other books.

Case

A book cover that is made completely before it is affixed to a book.

Casing-in

Pasting a book into its cover.

Cellulose Acetate Film Lamination

The fusing of sheets of cellulose acetate film to one or both sides of a piece of deacidified paper by means of heat and pressure. Tissue or another strong material is usually applied to the outer surfaces of the plastic film to increase the strength of the laminate; called also *archival lamination*.

Clasp

A hinged catch for holding together the two covers of a book.

Combination Press

A press that combines the functions of a number of presses as described in Klinefelter's book [21]. In this pamphlet: a press that serves as standing press, backing press, and casing-in press, having backing boards and brass-bound boards built into the upper and lower cheeks of the press.

Crash—See Super

Dust Cover, Jacket, or Wrapper—See Book Jacket

Edition Binding

The binding of an edition or a number of copies of the same book in identical style, usually by mass-production methods and in relatively large quantities, as opposed to hand binding or utility binding; also a book so bound which may be called a publisher's binding.

Enclosures

Any material not a part of the bound book which has been inserted into it. Pertinent enclosures are those which are somehow significantly related to the book (such as letters, clippings, reviews, pictures, etc.) and should be preserved as permanent inserts or stored separately.

End Paper

A folded sheet of paper of which one leaf is attached to a board of the book and the other forms a flyleaf; called also *end leaf, end sheet, end lining*. This term is also sometimes used to describe the leaf which is pasted down to the board, although, strictly speaking, this leaf should be referred to as the *board paper* or *pastedown*.

Ex Libris—*See* Bookplate

Felt Pads

Pieces of binder's board covered on both sides with felt.

Flag

A marker (such as a small strip of colored paper) placed to protrude from between the leaves of a book to show its shelf position, or to indicate that special attention should be given either to the whole book or to the page marked.

Flyleaf

A blank leaf at the beginning or end of a book; specifically: the free half of the end paper.

Folder

A piece of bone, shaped like a knife blade, used for folding sheets and in other binding processes.

Fore Edge

The edge of a book opposite the backbone.

Foxing

Freckle-like brownish spots that develop in paper under humid conditions if the paper contains iron particles or fungus, or both.

Gilt Edges

Book edges that have been covered with gold leaf and burnished.

Glassine Paper

A thin, dense, translucent paper which is resistant to the passage of air and grease.

Gutter

The white space formed by the adjoining inside margins of two facing pages; the inner margin of a book page.

Headband

In early or fine bindings, a strip of embroidery worked by hand at the head and tail of the backbone of the book; in most modern books, a strip of woven material glued on in those places.

Headcap

The covering leather that has been shaped over the headbands at the head and foot of the backbone of a hand-covered book.

Hinge

(*a*) A paper or muslin joint, stub, or guard in a bound book that strengthens or permits the free flexing of a section, insert, leaf, or map. (*b*) The flexible part of the binding material (leather, cloth, paper, etc.) on which the board opens. Also called *joint*.

Joint—See Hinge

Leaf

A sheet of paper (or of vellum), the two sides of which are pages of a book.

Leather

We have attempted to distinguish throughout this manual between alum-tawed leather and leather tanned by other means, because these two types of leather require different treatment. Wherever the word "leather" is used and it is not specifically stated, or clear from the context, that alum-tawed leather is meant, the word "leather" should be understood to mean leather prepared by any process other than alum-tawing. *See also* Alum-tawed Leather.

Lithographic Stone

A fine-grained dense slab of limestone prepared for lithography but used by bookbinders as a surface on which to pare leather or for other purposes.

Mull—See Super

Offset

Unintentional transfer of ink (as from the surface of a freshly printed sheet to the back of a sheet placed on top of it); also, the ink or image so transferred; called also *setoff*, especially in England, to distinguish the term from offset printing.

Oil, Oiling

Terms often used to describe a leather dressing which contains oil, and its application to leather bindings.

Page

A single side of the leaf of a book, newspaper, etc.

Parchment—See Vellum

Pastedown—See End Paper

Pressure-Sensitive Tape

The kind of pretreated tape that adheres to a surface when pressure is applied without the necessity of first applying adhesive or moistening or otherwise treating its surface.

Protective Container

A slipcase, telescoping box, solander case, or portfolio designed to contain and protect a book, pamphlet, or manuscript.

Protective Tissue

Thin tissue inserted to prevent an illustration from staining the opposite page.

Recto

The right-hand page of a book; usually carrying an odd page number.

Scalpel

A small, straight knife with a thin blade used especially in surgery.

Section

A sheet of paper consisting of two or more leaves folded and ready to be incorporated in the main body of the book. Called also *signature*.

Setoff—See Offset

Shelfback—See Backbone

Signature

May be used in place of the term "section." Also, the letter or figure sometimes placed at the bottom of the first page of each section of a book or pamphlet.

Sized Paper

Paper treated with a material that fills the pores of the surface so as to prevent or retard the penetration of liquids.

Slipcase

A protective container with one open end for books or other objects of similar shape and size; also called *slip cover*.

Spew

Material that exudes or is extruded. As: an oily or gummy exudate (as on the surface of leather). Also spelled *spue*.

Spine—See Backbone

Spue—See Spew

Square

Portion of binding cover that projects beyond leaves.

Standing Press

A vertical press in which printed and folded sheets and books are piled and pressed.

Super

A thin, loosely woven, open-meshed, starched cotton fabric used especially for reinforcing books. Also called *crash* or *mull*.

Tip

To affix or paste (an insert) in a book at the binding margin.

Turn-in

The covering material that is turned over the edges of a cover from the outside to the inside.

Vellum

An animal skin that has been treated with lime and stretched and scraped rather than tanned, used for writing and printing or for binding books. The skins are sometimes split (sliced horizontally into two layers), one layer of which is finished on both sides for use as a writing material. Such split skins, most commonly sheepskin, are called *parchment*. (The terms parchment and vellum are sometimes used interchangeably.)

Verso

The left-hand page of a book, usually carrying an even page number.

Wrapper—See Book Jacket

Selected Bibliography

1. Academy of Sciences of the USSR
   Laboratory for the Conservation and Restoration of Books
   New Methods for the Restoration and Preservation of Documents and Books
   Jerusalem, Israel Program for Scientific Translation, 1964
   Editor: N. ya. Solechnik.
   (Available from the Clearinghouse for Scientific and Technical Information, 5285 Port Royal Road, Springfield, Va. 22151)

   Topics covered include the use of high-frequency electromagnetic fields as a means of disinfecting books, the coating of paper with thermoplastic film, and the improvement of faded texts by photographic and radiographic methods.

2. BANKS, PAUL N.
   "Paper Cleaning"
   Copenhagen, *Restaurator*, v. 1, no. 1, 1969, pp. 52–66

   This article was one of six papers on "Paper: Composition, Deterioration, and Preservation" read at the annual meeting of the International Institute for the Conservation of Historic and Artistic Works—American Group, held in Chicago, June 6–8, 1966. Mr. Banks, the Conservator of the Newberry Library in Chicago, discusses dry, wet, and solvent methods of cleaning paper and the advantages and disadvantages of many of the methods of paper bleaching now in use. The paper was first printed in the *Journal of the Guild of Book Workers*, v. 5, no. 1, Fall, 1966, pp. 8–22, but has now been revised and updated for publication in the first issue of the first volume of this new journal on the preservation of library and archival material.

3. BARROW, W. J.
   Manuscripts and Documents: Their Deterioration and Restoration
   Charlottesville, Va., University of Virginia Press, 1955

   An account of the causes of paper decay and of a method to deacidify paper to help it to resist decay. The chapter on storage conditions discusses the deteriorating effects of polluted air, light rays, high temperatures, high humidity, migration, and insects and rodents.

4. BLADES, WILLIAM
The Enemies of Books; with a Preface by Richard Garnett. 3d ed.
London, Trubner, 1881

Blades discusses the following enemies of books (giving an interesting chapter to each subject): fire, water, gas and heat, dust and neglect, the bookworm, other vermin, incompetent bookbinders, and careless collectors. This book is of historical interest.

5. BUCK, MITCHELL S.
Book Repair and Restoration: A Manual of Practical Suggestions for Bibliophiles
Including some translated selections from Essai sur l'art de Restaurer les Estampes et les Livres, par A. Bonnardot, Paris, 1858; Philadelphia, Nicholas L. Brown, 1918

The author discusses general restoration, removing stains, rebacking, repairing old bindings, and rebinding.

6. CHURCH, A. H.
"Destruction of Leather by Gas"
London, *Chemical News*, v. 36, p. 179, 1877

States that sulphuric acid in coal gas causes leather to deteriorate. Books on the upper shelves deteriorated faster than those on the lower shelves. Deteriorated books contained free sulphuric acid.

7. CLOUGH, ERIC A.
Bookbinding for Librarians
London, Association of Assistant Librarians, 1957

The only recent book in English which attempts to cover the field of binding for libraries in a comprehensive manner. It contains much information about all aspects of this subject. The fact that many of the practices discussed vary from those used in America should not deter American librarians from studying the book, as many British library binding practices are superior to the American ones. The chapter entitled "Recent Developments," however, must be read with caution, as some of the materials discussed are not safe for use in connection with paper.

8. COCKERELL, DOUGLAS
Bookbinding and the Care of Books
London, Pitman, 5th ed., 1955

This is the classic work on hand binding. Part II discusses the injurious influences to which books are subject, proper shelving, insect pests, how to preserve old bindings, and the rebacking of books. The chapter on leather quotes generously from the Report of the Committee on Leather Bookbinding published for the Society of Arts in 1905.

9. COCKERELL, DOUGLAS
   Some Notes on Bookbinding
   London, Oxford University Press, 1929

   Discusses the deterioration of the quality of materials used in bindings and gives interesting historical and sociological reasons for its occurrence.

10. COCKERELL, SYDNEY M.
    The Repairing of Books
    London, Sheppard Press, 1958

    Librarians and collectors will find this an interesting summary of some of the possible ways in which books can be repaired. To quote the author: "It contains some 'first aid' operations that can be carried out by careful labour, but it is not a technical work on binding procedure, nor is it intended to give the impression that anyone can repair a valuable book without practical instruction and experience; and it is hoped that this experience will not be obtained at the expense of fine books."

11. CORDEROY, JOHN
    Bookbinding for Beginners
    London, Studio Vista; New York, Watson-Guptill, 1967.

    Although this little manual on bookbinding suffers from the same defect as many such manuals, that is, not enough detail, the information given is eminently sensible and useful, making it the best of its kind.

12. CUNHA, GEORGE DANIEL MARTIN
    Conservation of Library Materials; A Manual and Bibliography on the Care, Repair and Restoration of Library Materials
    Metuchen, N.J., Scarecrow Press, 1967

    Although the organization of the material is often confusing, this book is the only one of its kind in the field. The author, who is the Conservator of the Library of the Boston Athenaeum, discusses the nature, general care, and repair and restoration of library materials. The bibliography is extensive.

13. DUHMERT, ANNELIESE
    Buchpflege: Eine Bibliographie
    Stuttgart, Max Hettler Verlag, 1963

    Though poorly edited, this is the most comprehensive bibliography on the subject of the care of books.

14. FELLER, ROBERT L.
"Control of Deteriorating Effects of Light upon Museum Objects"
Museum, 1964, XVII, No. 2, pp. 57–98

    Includes a comprehensive bibliography on the subject.

15. GRANT, JULIUS
Books and Documents: Dating, Permanence and Preservation
London, Grafton, 1937

    Gives a good history of bookmaking, especially of paper.

16. GREATHOUSE, GLENN A., AND CARL J. WESSEL
Deterioration of Materials: Causes and Preventive Techniques
A collaboration under the joint auspices of the Services Technical Committee of Department of Defense and the Prevention of Deterioration Center Division of Chemistry and Chemical Technology. National Academy of Sciences–National Research Council
New York, Reinhold Publishing Corporation, 1954

    Librarians will find the chapters on "Factors in Deterioration" and "Materials and Their Preservation" of interest.

17. HARRISON, L. S.
Report on the Deteriorating Effects of Modern Light Sources
New York, Metropolitan Museum of Art, 1954

    An excellent report on the subject. It is only very recently that the causes of the harmful effects of artificial light have been the subject of exhaustive scientific study.

18. HULME, E. WYNDHAM, AND OTHERS
Leather for Libraries
London, Library Supply Company, 1905

    An important summary of the history of the degeneration in the quality of leather, with recommendations for proper tanning techniques to produce lasting leather.

19. INNES, R. F.
"The Preservation of Vegetable-tanned Leather against Deterioration"
Chapter 18 in *Progress in Leather Science*
London, British Leather Manufacturers' Research Association, pp. 426–50, 1948

    A pioneering work in the explanation of the causes of the decay of leather and its prevention. The author discusses preferred tannages, considering pyrogallol-tanned better than catechol-tanned hides, and confirms that salts added to leather increase its durability. Potassium citrate or lactate as well as neutralized syntans protect the leather. Alum retannage and an impermeable finish also improve durability.

20. INTERNATIONAL CENTRE FOR THE STUDY OF THE PRESERVATION AND THE RESTORATION OF CULTURAL PROPERTY
Synthetic Materials used in the Conservation of Cultural Property
Rome, The Centre, 1963

An extremely useful little book, which describes the characteristics of various categories of synthetic materials—varnishes, plastic sheets, adhesives, consolidants, and similar materials—in terms of their chemical composition, their stability, and their uses. Also included are indices of trade names of synthetic materials and of their manufacturers.

21. KLINEFELTER, LEE M.
Bookbinding Made Easy
New York, The Bruce Publishing Company, Rev. ed., 1960

Mr. Klinefelter includes many interesting diagrams of bookbinding equipment which can be made at home. Among his diagrams is one on page 8 which he calls Figure 7, Gluing Press. The Combination Press mentioned in the Supply and Equipment List and described on page 31 is a variation of this press.

22. LANGWELL, W. H.
The Conservation of Books and Documents
London, Pitman, 1957

Chapters on the early history of papermaking; modern paper; causes of damage to paper; prevention of damage to paper, parchment and vellum, inks, sewing materials, adhesives, other bookbinding materials; techniques; with a bibliography and index.

23. LeGEAR, H. M.
Maps: Their Care, Repair and Preservation in Libraries
Washington, Library of Congress, 1950

Out of print, but now available in facsimile form from University Microfilms, A Xerox Company, 300 North Zeeb Road, Ann Arbor, Michigan 48106. This excellent book covers the subjects of the processing, care, repair, preservation, and storage of maps.

24. LEHMANN-HAUPT, HELLMUT
"On the Rebinding of Old Books"
In *Bookbinding in America: Three Essays* (H. Lehmann-Haupt, ed.)
New York, R. R. Bowker Company, Rev. ed., 1967

This book is made up of three parts. The first part, by Hannah French, gives the best account of the history of hand bookbinding in

America from 1636 to 1820. The second part, written by Joseph W. Rogers, covers the rise of American edition binding. The third part, by Lehmann-Haupt, is a sound, thoughtful, and very useful discussion of the ethics and esthetics of rebinding books of value.

25. LEIGHTON, JOHN
"On the Library, Books and Binding, Particularly with Regard to Their Restoration and Preservation"
London, *Royal Society of Arts, Journal*, 1858–59, v. 7, pp. 209–15; Discussion, pp. 215–19

The decay of leather was attributed by the author to excessive heat, the sulphur fumes in coal gas which oxidized into sulphuric acid, improper tanning, the use of oxalic acid by bookbinders, impurities in the adhesives, and the action of light.

26. V. I. LENIN LIBRARY
The Hygiene and Restoration of Books in the City Library
Hygiene, by C. I. Kornaeva
Restoration, by N. A. Chermeecina
Editor, O. V. Kozulina
Moscow, 1960

This comprehensive book describes Soviet methods of cleaning and preserving paper and bindings and of controlling insects and mold.

27. LODEVIJKS, X. J.
"The Influence of Light on Museum Objects"
In *Recent Advances in Conservation* (G. Thomson, ed.). London, Butterworth, 1963, pp. 7–8

Discusses photochemical decay caused by ultraviolet radiation and other light rays and urges the reduction of the intensity of light as well as the avoidance of artificial lighting which contains short waves.

28. LYDENBERG, HARRY MILLER, AND JOHN ARCHER
Revised by John Alden
The Care and Repair of Books
New York, R. R. Bowker Company, 1960

This book contains chapters on the enemies of books, repair and mending, treatment of paper, vellum, leather, and cloth, and a comprehensive bibliography. The authors, however, encourage the readers to attempt repairs which even a trained binder should hesitate to attempt, such as the restoration of papyrus, oriental, or palm-leaf manuscripts.

29. MIDDLETON, BERNARD C.
A History of English Craft Bookbinding Technique
New York and London, Hafner Publishing Company, 1963

   As the title suggests, this excellent book is a history of the technique of bookbinding and is therefore useful to book curators in dating bindings.

30. MINOGUE, ADELAIDE E.
The Repair and Preservation of Records
Bulletins of the National Archives, No. 5, September, 1943
Washington, D.C.

   Although out of print, this pamphlet is worth consulting. It gives an excellent summary of the causes and prevention of decay, and the cleaning and repair of bindings, seals, parchments, and maps.

31. NEW YORK STATE LIBRARY. LIBRARY EXTENSION DIVISION
Your Book Collection: Its Care
Albany, N.Y., New York State Library, 1957

   Discusses the physical appearance and appeal of a collection as a whole.

32. PLENDERLEITH, H. J.
The Conservation of Antiquities and Works of Art: Treatment, Repair, and Restoration
London, Oxford University Press, 1956

   This is the basic reference work used by conservators in the museum as well as in the library field. There are excellent and useful chapters on the causes of decay and the treatment of animal skins, papyrus, and paper.

33. PLENDERLEITH, H. J.
The Preservation of Leather Bookbindings
London, British Museum, 1947

   First published in 1946, but we cite the 1947 edition because of its corrected formula for leather protection. Based on results of investigations initiated by the British Leather Manufacturers' Association, Plenderleith acknowledges the work of R. Faraday Innes: "His discoveries in regard to the mechanism and prevention of decay have provided data for the solution of library problems which have defied interpretation for years. He has established a simple condition under which vegetable tanned leather remains permanently free from chemical decay even when containing sulphuric acid."

34. ROGERS, J. S., AND C. W. BEEBE
Leather Bookbindings: How To Preserve Them
Leaflet No. 398, United States Department of Agriculture
Washington, D.C., May, 1956

The latest government bulletin about the preservation of leather bindings. Eight formulas are given.

35. ROYAL SOCIETY OF ARTS, LONDON
Report of the Committee on Leather for Bookbinding
Edited for the Society of Arts and the Company of Leathersellers by the Rt. Hon. Viscount Cobham and Sir Henry Trueman Wood
London, published for the Society of Arts by George Bell & Sons, 1905

Amplification of the report in 1901 which is quoted in Cockerell's *Bookbinding and the Care of Books.*

36. SANTUCCI, LUDOVICO
"The Application of Chemical and Physical Methods to Conservation of Archival Materials"
In *Recent Advances in Conservation* (G. Thomson, ed.)
London, Butterworth, 1963, pp. 39–47

A comprehensive survey of progress in the field of archival conservation. The extensive bibliography does not give the titles of articles in journals, making it less useful than it otherwise would be.

37. SPAWN, WILLMAN
"The Conservation of Books and Papers"
Ontario Library Review, February, 1962

An abridgment of a more detailed manuscript written by the resident Book Restorer at the American Philosophical Society.

38. SPEYERS-DURAN, PETER
Moving Library Materials
Chicago, Library Technology Project, American Library Association, Rev. ed., 1965

Although this pamphlet deals with moving books from one building to another, it presents many interesting ideas about the handling of books when they are off the shelf.

39. STORM, COLTON
"Care, Maintenance, and Restoration"
In *Rare Book Collections* (H. Richard Archer, ed.)
Chicago, ACRL Monograph No. 27, ALA, 1965

A statement of principles of the conservation of rare materials rather than a manual on the subject.

40. TRIBOLET, HAROLD W.
"Trends in Preservation"
Library Trends, Vol. 13, No. 2, University of Illinois Graduate School of Library Science, October, 1964

Mr. Tribolet, manager of the Department of Extra Binding at R. R. Donnelley & Sons Co. in Chicago, discusses recent developments in the treatment of rare books and manuscripts.

41. THE USSR STATE LIBRARY IM. V. I. LENIN
Department for Book Preservation and Restoration
Collection of Materials on the Preservation of Library Resources
Jerusalem, Israel Program for Scientific Translations, 1964
No. 2, L. Petrova, ed.; No. 3, L. Belyakova and O. V. Kozulina, eds.

This work includes chapters on inspecting book collections, dusting and cleaning books, and softening leather bindings.

42. WALTON, ROBERT P.
Causes and Prevention of Deterioration in Book Materials
New York, New York Public Library, 1929

A bibliography with extensive abstracts, covering the following subjects: preservation and durability of book papers, deterioration of bookbinding leathers, leather-preservative compositions, and the determination of acidity in leathers. Includes an author index. Under each heading the references are listed chronologically, which makes this publication a capsule history of each subject.

43. WATSON, ALDREN
Hand Bookbinding: A Manual of Instruction
New York, Reinhold Publishing Corporation, 1963

This book, written and illustrated by the illustrator of this manual, covers such subjects as the making of dust jackets, single-signature books, manuscript, case and sheet music binding, the making of boxes and slipcases and of tools and equipment for binding. The illustrations are outstandingly explicit.

44. ZIGROSSER, CARL, AND CHRISTA M. GAEHDE
A Guide to the Collecting and Care of Original Prints
Sponsored by The Print Council of America
New York, Crown Publishers, Inc., 1965

Many of the authors' suggestions for the care of prints may also be applied to the care of maps, broadsides, etc.

Index

This pamphlet was printed and bound by American Publishers Press,
Chicago, Illinois. The type face used is Monotype Bembo;
the process offset lithography. The text and cover papers are
"Permalife," a stable, durable paper made by the
Standard Paper Manufacturing Company, Richmond, Virginia.
The specifications for this type of paper were developed under a grant
from the Council on Library Resources, Inc.